Faithful Questions

Exploring the Way with Jesus

© 2015 by Forward Movement

ISBN 978-0-88028-420-2

Forward Movement
412 Sycamore Street
Cincinnati, Ohio USA 45202

Faithful Questions: Exploring the Way with Jesus is a companion to the *Transforming Questions* course, which has been supported by a generous grant from The Episcopal Church's Constable Fund.

www.forwardmovement.org

Faithful Questions

Exploring the Way with Jesus

Scott Gunn and Melody Wilson Shobe

Forward Movement

Cincinnati, Ohio

TABLE OF CONTENTS

INTRODUCTION

Some years ago, I met with parents and godparents on a Saturday as we prepared for their child's baptism the next morning. We went through the service, and I talked with them about baptism and what it means. It was a wonderful couple of hours as we discussed the joys and challenges of raising a child in the Christian faith.

That night, about 10:30, my phone rang. One of the godparents was on the other end. "We took the service leaflet home, and I was reading through it. I'm not sure I can go through with this tomorrow morning." I asked her to say more. "These promises seem impossible, and I'm not really sure I can say I believe every single word that I'm supposed to say."

What a gift to have this conversation as a priest! I explained to this worried godparent that no godparent or parent had called me with a similar question in all the baptisms I had ever celebrated as a priest, and I was especially glad she had called. I reassured her, saying that our task as Christians isn't to be theological experts but rather to commit to our life in Christ. Our job is to explore, to ask questions, to grow in faith. I told her that I thought she would be an exceptionally good godparent, because she was doing the thing that I hope every Christian would do: go on a great journey of exploration and growth, even when we are unsure where that journey will take us.

As we ended our call, I explained that the questions and promises we make are not ours alone. We make extravagant promises, but we do so with a terrific answer. "I will, with God's help." God promises to be with us, and in that, we can find great strength.

Whether we are new Christians or longtime Christians, wrestling with our faith is part of the journey. Anyone who engages both brain and heart will sometimes be torn. Why doesn't God answer all prayers? How can we profess faith in things that seem scientifically impossible? Do real Christians doubt?

It is our strong belief that doubt is the companion of faith. As you will read in the coming pages, the big names in the Bible almost all had questions for God at one time or another. Nearly every saint in Christian history struggled at times. Contrary to what might seem obvious, a lack of struggle is not a sign of a healthy faith journey. If we don't have big questions, it's usually because we are not taking our faith seriously. Or perhaps we are not taking our brain seriously.

To proclaim the idea that Jesus was raised from the dead, for example, is an astounding claim. Jesus' own disciples—the people who had seen miracle after miracle—had trouble accepting the glad news of Easter morning. We should be gentle with ourselves if we, too, grapple with our faith—and our questions.

This book is an effort to assure you that questions are part of the journey and to equip you with tools and courage to explore the Christian faith. We will discuss how to ask questions faithfully, in ways that provide opportunities for growth and transformation. We will see that asking deep questions can lead to deep faith. And we will look at some tools for our journey of exploration.

How to use this book

There are several ways to use this book. You might like to read it through and reflect on some of the suggestion questions at the end of each chapter. Or perhaps you will gather with a few others and read it together, using the questions as the basis for discussion and exploration.

Faithful Questions is a companion to a course offered by Forward Movement called *Transforming Questions*. That course is offered over ten sessions, with an instructor offering talks based on an outline. This book is very much like the outline an instructor for *Transforming Questions* might use. So you could read this book while you take the class, or if you are the instructor, it might help you prepare to lead the sessions.

We suggest you read the book with a Bible nearby, if you can. Chapter 5 will help you choose a Bible if you don't have one you love. Throughout the book, there are scripture references to look up if you'd like to go deeper. You can always type the scripture references into Google and read them on the Internet, if you don't have a printed Bible handy.

In the back of the book, there are some suggested resources to use in further exploration. You might also visit the website www.transformingquestions.org for additional resources.

A note from the authors

You will read lots of first-person stories in *Faithful Questions*. Sometimes the "I" is Melody, and sometimes it is Scott. Don't worry too much about who is speaking. Just savor the story!

Many of the ideas in this book come from our time of working, worshiping, and teaching together as priests on the staff of an Episcopal congregation in Rhode Island. There, we saw lives transformed through the pages of scripture and the journey of thoughtful exploration. We hope this will happen for you as well. May God bless you with curiosity, wonder, joy, courage, strength, and faith.

Scott Gunn   Melody Wilson Shobe
Cincinnati, Ohio   Dallas, Texas

The Feast of Julian of Norwich, 2015

CAN I QUESTION
MY FAITH?

O God, by whom the meek are guided in judgment, and light rises up in darkness for the godly: Grant us, in all our doubts and uncertainties, the grace to ask what you would have us to do, that the Spirit of wisdom may save us from all false choices, and that in your light we may see light, and in your straight path may not stumble; through Jesus Christ our Lord. Amen.

(*The Book of Common Prayer*, p. 832)

Many Christians and seekers operate under the mistaken assumption that doubt is the opposite of faith. Sometimes we hear people say that to have faith means accepting things without questioning them. Others say that you can't be a "good Christian" if you have a lot of doubt. Nothing could be further from the truth. In fact, questions are an essential part of faith.

Almost every single person in scripture who encounters God does so with a lot of questions—and more than a little doubt. Let's look at an example from the story of Abraham and Sarah, a faithful couple who were the forebearers of our faith. As this story begins, Abraham and Sarah have already had extraordinary encounters with God. Still, when God tells Abraham that he and Sarah will have a son, Sarah laughs at the very idea. She laughs—because it seems utterly impossible to become pregnant at her advanced age—and then she goes on to deny her doubt and her laughter. God knows about her doubt and still God blesses Sarah and Abraham with a child. The point is that even these people—who had known God through conversation, encounter, and miracle—had doubts.

Abraham and Sarah
Genesis 18:1-15

The LORD appeared to Abraham by the oaks of Mamre, as he sat at the entrance of his tent in the heat of the day. He looked up and saw three men standing near him. When he saw them, he ran from the tent entrance to meet them, and bowed down to the ground. He said, "My lord, if I find favor with you, do not pass by your servant. Let a little water be brought, and wash your feet, and rest yourselves under the tree. Let me bring a little bread, that you may refresh yourselves, and after that you may pass on—since you have come to your servant." So they said, "Do as you have said." And Abraham hastened into the tent to Sarah, and said, "Make ready quickly three measures of choice flour, knead it, and make cakes." Abraham ran to the herd, and took a calf, tender and good, and gave it to the servant, who hastened to prepare it. Then he took curds and milk and the calf that he had prepared, and set it before them; and he stood by them under the tree while they ate.

They said to him, "Where is your wife Sarah?" And he said, "There, in the tent." Then one said, "I will surely return to you in due season, and your wife Sarah shall have a son." And Sarah was listening at the tent entrance behind him. Now Abraham and Sarah were old, advanced in age; it had ceased to be with Sarah after the manner of women. So Sarah laughed to herself, saying, "After I have grown old, and my husband is old, shall I have pleasure?" The LORD said to Abraham, "Why did Sarah laugh, and say, 'Shall I indeed bear a child, now that I am old?' Is anything too wonderful for the LORD? At the set time I will return to you, in due season, and Sarah shall have a son." But Sarah denied, saying, "I did not laugh"; for she was afraid. He said, "Oh yes, you did laugh."

Sarah and Abraham are not the only faithful people who doubt God; there are lots of other examples. Moses has many questions for God (Exodus 3:4-15; 4:1-17) as he is called to be a leader of God's people. In fact, the whole story of Moses is one long series of episodes of

> ### QUESTIONS IN THE PSALMS
>
> Psalm 22:1
> Psalm 13:1-2
> Psalm 44:23-26
> Psalm 121:1
> Psalm 139:7

doubt and faith among God, Moses, and God's people. Despite their doubts, God remains faithful to the people.

The psalms are full of doubts and questions. Perhaps the most famous question in the psalter is one that Jesus quoted as he was hanging on the cross, "My God, my God, why have you forsaken me? Why are you so far from helping me, from the words of my groaning?" (Psalm 22:1). This psalm begins as a lament, asking why God seems so far from human suffering but then eventually moves to a place of confident faith. Again and again in the psalms, we hear voices of faithful people crying out to God with their questions, confronting God with their doubts.

In the New Testament, there are even more questions; many of them come from the people closest to Jesus: his disciples and followers. But the most famous story of doubt in the New Testament must surely be that of Thomas encountering Jesus in the Upper Room, the episode that earned him the nickname "Doubting Thomas."

QUESTIONING DISCIPLES

Mary
(Luke 1:26-38)

Nicodemus
(John 3:1-12 and John 19:38-42)

Paul
(Acts 22:6-16)

Thomas Doubts
John 20:24-29

But Thomas (who was called the Twin), one of the twelve, was not with them when Jesus came. So the other disciples told him, "We have seen the Lord." But he said to them, "Unless I see the mark of the nails in his hands, and put my finger in the mark of the nails and my hand in his side, I will not believe."

A week later his disciples were again in the house, and Thomas was with them. Although the doors were shut, Jesus came and stood among them and said, "Peace be with you." Then he said to

Thomas, "Put your finger here and see my hands. Reach out your hand and put it in my side. Do not doubt but believe." Thomas answered him, "My Lord and my God!" Jesus said to him, "Have you believed because you have seen me? Blessed are those who have not seen and yet have come to believe."

Thomas was away when Jesus had appeared to the disciples the first time, and so he quite naturally had questions about whether the Jesus the others claimed to have seen was

Thomas immediately believes, an inspiring example of faith overcoming doubt.

real. If someone told you a dead person had appeared, would you believe it?! So Thomas expresses his doubt, and when Jesus appears later, he invites Thomas to touch his wounds and verify that he has, indeed, been raised from the dead. Thomas immediately believes, crying out, "My Lord and my God!"—an inspiring example of faith overcoming doubt. This is, for us, a fitting example. We have doubts; they are only natural. We should ask our questions, probing deeper into our faith. But we should also be ready to believe, to be transformed. Poor Thomas gets a bad rap when he is called "Doubting Thomas." For his courage in asking the questions, I wish Thomas were instead called "Good Question Thomas." Perhaps

CAN I QUESTION MY FAITH?

then we would all be more ready faithfully to ask our questions, and through asking them, be transformed.

Jesus was constantly challenging people to change, to be transformed.

I could offer many examples of faithful people in the scriptures who had moments of doubt. In fact, it would be hard to find people who didn't experience doubts and questions in their encounters with God. Do you see a pattern though? Faithful people have extraordinary encounters. They raise their questions, and then they proceed in faith and in confidence.

Asking and wrestling with questions is how we stay in relationship. We bring our thoughts, our concerns, our questions, and our struggles to God, believing that what God has to say about them is important. It is precisely in asking questions that it becomes possible for us to grow and to develop in our faith.

Jesus never encountered people and told them to "stay just as you are." He was constantly challenging people to change, to be transformed. We Christians are disciples— that word comes from Greek and means "students"—of Jesus. We disciples, like all students, are meant to ask questions, knowing that through questions, we learn. The process of asking these questions and exploring the answers is how we learn about ourselves, about one another, and most especially about God.

This shouldn't come as a surprise to Episcopalians. Our *Book of Common Prayer* has a Catechism—a teaching tool for our faith—in a question and answer format. You can see the Catechism on page 845 of the prayer book, and it's an excellent example of how we ask questions and then hear answers that lead to further questions— questions that can lead us on a path to a deeper faith.

Yet sometimes we move to the opposite extreme. Rather than being afraid to ask questions, we ask them in a way that undermines our faith. We ask questions in ways that are not faithful but combative. We ask questions not to encounter God or other Christians but to trip up God or others. Sometimes people say that anything goes, that Christians don't believe any specific things. They say that we ask an endless series of questions, but we're not interested in answers or in exploration. That's not what faithful questioning looks like.

Perhaps the best example of faithful questioning in the Bible is the story of Jacob in Genesis 32.

Jacob Wrestles at Peniel
Genesis 32:22-31

The same night he got up and took his two wives, his two maids, and his eleven children, and crossed the ford of the Jabbok. He took them and sent them across the stream, and likewise everything that he had. Jacob was left alone; and a man wrestled with him until daybreak. When the man saw that he did not prevail against Jacob, he struck him on the hip socket; and Jacob's hip was put out of joint as he wrestled with him. Then he said, "Let me go, for the day is breaking." But Jacob said, "I will not let you go, unless you bless me." So he said to him, "What is your name?" And he said, "Jacob." Then the man said, "You shall no longer be called Jacob, but Israel, for you have striven with God and with humans, and have prevailed." Then Jacob asked him, "Please tell me your name." But he said, "Why is it that you ask my name?" And there he blessed him. So Jacob called the place Peniel, saying, "For I have seen God face to face, and yet my life is preserved." The sun rose upon him as he passed Penuel, limping because of his hip.

Jacob had left the house of his father-in-law, and he was headed back to face his brother, whom he had tricked and deceived the last time they met. That night, he stayed alone by the river Jabbok "and a man wrestled with him until daybreak." Jewish tradition has long held that Jacob was wrestling an angel rather than a mere mortal. Jacob himself seemed to think he had wrestled with God; he said after the encounter that he had seen God face to face.

All night long, Jacob wrestled with this representative of God. And as he wrestled, he asked questions. Jacob asked God for his name. Jacob asked for a blessing. All night long, Jacob wrestled God, holding God close, in spite of exhaustion and frustration. He didn't let go.

Faithful questioning is wrestling.

That kind of wrestling is exactly what faithful questioning of God looks like. It isn't lobbing questions like missiles from a distance, seeing if they hit the mark and never looking for a response. It isn't letting go, walking away, and saying none of it matters. It's not a hands-off, no-contact, long-distance activity.

Faithful questioning is wrestling. It's sweat and breath and blood—up close and personal. It's clinging tightly, as though your life depends on it, as though it really matters. It's not letting go, in spite of exhaustion and frustration and pain.

Jacob wrestles all night long, and in the end, he doesn't even get his answers. Instead he gets a new name, a new identity: Israel, which means "one who strives with God." Jacob's willingness to cling to God in the midst of unanswered questions, to hold on and not to let go, becomes his central, defining identity. And from Jacob—from Israel—comes the people Israel, the people understood as belonging to God in a special way. The pattern for faithfulness, for being people of God, starts with a wrestling match! God's people are called to be God's wrestlers. We are called to be willing to ask questions, to encounter God, and never to let go, no matter what.

So as Christians, the dilemma is not whether or not we should or can ask questions. We should, we can, we must! Our dilemma is exploring how we ask questions about our faith. How do we ask questions of God? And what sources help us to wrestle with these questions and create the possibility of finding answers, of further exploration?

There are three important principles for asking questions faithfully as Christians.

We ask questions **in community**.

Malcolm Gladwell, in his book *David and Goliath*, tells about a series of studies on ideal class size in schools. In those studies, they learned that while a class that was too large was detrimental, so also was a class that was too small. This is partly because, in a class, students learn not only from the teacher but also from each other.

This is fundamentally true in the life of faith as well. From the beginning, Jewish rabbis gathered in groups for teaching and debate. There were twelve disciples. The earliest Christians gathered to worship, to pray, and to learn as a community. As people of faith, we learn by asking questions together. It reminds us that we are not alone, that all faithful Christians in all times and in all places have questions and doubts. It helps us to seek and to find support in the process of discovering God and growing in our faith. We learn from one another. At times we inspire one another, at times we share insights with one another, and at times we share our doubts with one another.

We ask questions **of God**, believing that God is big enough for our questions.

If we aren't asking our questions of God, then we are turning only to other sources (culture, our own brains, and so on). While those sources aren't necessarily bad, they are limited, and they're not the corresponding sources for our questions. You wouldn't consult a math textbook for an answer to a history question or observe the stars to learn how to knit. Our questions about faith and about God are rightly addressed to God.

We ask questions, consulting **a variety of sources**.

In our tradition as Anglican Christians, we don't believe that there's one-stop shopping for the answers to our questions (if answers are to be found). It's not enough to quote one isolated verse of the Bible. It's not enough to say, "the church has always done it that way." It's not enough to say, "I feel like this is the right thing."

As Episcopalians, as Anglicans, we believe that we are called to consult at least three sources, together, as we explore questions: scripture, tradition, and reason. This is the famous three-legged stool of Anglicanism, and you know what happens if one leg is weak: the stool collapses. Both our questions and our answers are likely to be nuanced and complex; so too the sources we explore may be rich. It is how our sources are in conversation with one another that help us discover what God is saying, how God is calling us. We do this so that our answers—and our very questions—are balanced and rich.

Throughout this book, we will ask a lot of questions. This process is not the opposite of faith, but rather it is part and parcel of what it means to be faithful. As you continue reading this book, bring along your questions and doubts, knowing you are not alone in them. Be prepared to wrestle with the questions in ways that will be both enlivening and difficult. Be ready to discover surprising things. Sometimes an answer will be more difficult and demanding than you had hoped. Sometimes an answer might be simpler and more surprising than you thought possible. Sometimes answers lead to more questions, raising a rock and finding beneath it a teeming mass of wormy questions demanding deeper engagement. Most importantly, know that you always have company in your questions. You have God's abiding presence, and you have the company of other Christians who stand ready to explore with you. God is ready to hear your questions, even the ones offered only in the silence of our hearts. Christians are ready to walk with you, to challenge you in your questions and in your thoughts.

So perhaps we ought not to be asking if we can ask questions of our faith but rather how we can question faithfully.

In the Gospel of Mark, we hear this story of a father who brings his son to Jesus to seek healing.

The Healing of a Boy with a Spirit
Mark 9:22-25

Jesus asked the father, "How long has this been happening to him?" And he said, "From childhood. It has often cast him into the fire and into the water, to destroy him; but if you are able to do anything, have pity on us and help us." Jesus said to him, "If you are able!—All things can be done for the one who believes." Immediately the father of the child cried out, "I believe; help my unbelief!" When Jesus saw that a crowd came running together, he rebuked the unclean spirit, saying to it, "You spirit that keeps this boy from speaking and hearing, I command you, come out of him, and never enter him again!"

In the depths of despair, a father cries out to Jesus, "If you are able to do anything, have pity on us and help us." That "if" is the difficult part. It is the tinge of doubt in the midst of faith; though the father has brought his son to Jesus in desperation, he isn't really certain that it will be effective. If we are honest, it is the same "if" that we often feel when we approach God: believing, but doubting; knowing, yet questioning; convicted, but not convinced. As we explore our faith and wrestle with our questions, perhaps we can do no better than the prayer of this father, our fellow doubter: "Lord, I believe, help thou mine unbelief" (Mark 9:24, King James Version).

Almighty and eternal God, so draw our hearts to you, so guide our minds, so fill our imaginations, so control our wills, that we may be wholly yours, utterly dedicated to you; and then use us, we pray you, as you will, and always to your glory and the welfare of your people; through our Lord and Savior Jesus Christ. Amen.

(*The Book of Common Prayer*, pp. 832-3)

Reflection questions

The Bible is full of stories of faithful people who question God. Read the story of Nicodemus (John 3:1-12; 19:38-42). Explore the following questions:

❖ What kinds of questions is Nicodemus asking?

❖ Does he receive answers to his questions?

❖ How does asking questions impact his faith and actions?

❖ What in Nicodemus's story do you identify with?

❖ How does his story challenge you?

❖ What questions do you have?

❖ Have you ever been reluctant to ask your questions of faith? Why or why not?

WHO IS JESUS?

Almighty God, whom truly to know is everlasting life: Grant us so perfectly to know your Son Jesus Christ to be the way, the truth, and the life, that we may steadfastly follow his steps in the way that leads to eternal life; through Jesus Christ your Son our Lord, who lives and reigns with you, in the unity of the Holy Spirit, one God, for ever and ever. Amen.

(*The Book of Common Prayer*, p. 225)

Perhaps the fundamental question of our faith as Christians is: Who is Jesus? After all, we bear Jesus' very name in what we call ourselves—"Christ"-ians, those who follow Christ. So it makes sense that to understand what it means to be a Christian, we must first understand who is this Christ, this Jesus, for whom we have named ourselves. To know who Jesus is, we have to move past our postcard image of Jesus Christ, the familiar Jesus of our upbringing or of popular culture.

When I was growing up, part of my education encouraged me to learn about the great art of Western civilization. My classes taught me just a little about music, literature, painting, drama, and sculpture. I was especially captivated by some of the ancient sculptures. How could lifeless marble show us so much about life? The Venus de Milo (Aphrodite of Milos) is certainly one of the most famous sculptures. Though the ravages of time have not been kind to her, the sculpture still conveys stirring beauty and elegance.

A few years ago, I had a chance to visit The Louvre in Paris. Some recess in my mind remembered that the Venus de Milo is displayed there, and so when I got to the museum, I went to her gallery almost immediately. She is stunning, displayed in the center of a large room. What happened next is a bit, well, embarrassing. All the pictures I had ever seen showed her looking into the camera. But of course, the Venus de Milo is a sculpture in three dimensions. In this large room, I could walk all around her. I saw her sides and her back, parts I had neither seen nor considered before. The sculpture is even more stunning than

Two-dimensional pictures did not do this three-dimensional sculpture justice.

I had imagined. Two-dimensional pictures did not do justice to this three-dimensional sculpture.

Sometimes I think our encounter with Jesus Christ is a little like my encounter with Venus. We learn a particular view, and even though we might think we know better, we see Jesus only one way. We don't realize that there are lots of perspectives. Sometimes you have to walk around a bit to see the whole thing. We have to go on a journey.

This isn't to say that anything goes. As I walked around the Venus de Milo that day, I saw her from many perspectives. But I wasn't looking into the other rooms and confusing nearby sculptures with Venus. Rather, my view of this sculpture was literally expanded by my encounter. So too our view of Jesus might be expanded as we journey.

Many reasonable people—not only Christians but also Jews, Muslims, and others—believe that a man called Jesus Christ lived. In fact, a fair amount of historical evidence supports the case that Jesus Christ really lived.

So we can begin answering the question of "Who is Jesus?" by exploring some of what we know from history.

Josephus, born in 37 CE (just a few years after Jesus died and was raised) wrote:

> Now there was about this time Jesus, a wise man, if it be lawful to call him a man; for he was a doer of wonderful works, a teacher of such men as receive the truth with pleasure. He drew over to him both many of the Jews and many of the Gentiles. He was [the] Christ. And when Pilate, at the suggestion of the principal men amongst us, had condemned him to the cross, those that loved him at the first did not forsake him; for he appeared to them alive again the third day; as the divine prophets had foretold these and ten thousand other wonderful things concerning him. And the tribe of Christians, so named from him, are not extinct at this day. (*Antiquities of the Jews*)

Along with these non-Christian historians who lived close to the time of Jesus, we have the witness of the scriptures. Most scholars of ancient texts—even those who are not believing Christians—agree that the documents of the New Testament are themselves quite ancient, dating as early as twenty years after the time of Jesus. Several sources offer evidence that Jesus lived.

Most people today, regardless of their faith, agree to the fact that Jesus lived. Even non-Christians can agree that Jesus lived and that he did many good

> Jesus Christ was not only human but also was and is fully divine.

deeds; in fact lots of people see Jesus as a "good teacher." Some people—some Jews and all Muslims—go farther and say that Jesus was a prophet, someone who spoke for God; this is the way that Jesus is described throughout the *Qur'an*, the holy book of Islam. Everyone who agrees that Jesus lived will also agree that he died. But this is where Christians make a unique claim: Jesus lived and died—AND he was raised to new life. Jesus Christ, we Christians say, was not only human but also was and is fully divine.

How do we get from understanding Jesus as others do—as someone who was a good person, perhaps a prophet, as someone who lived and died—to understanding Jesus as Christianity does, that Jesus was not only a good

SOURCES MENTIONING JESUS

Josephus
(born 37 CE)

Tacitus
(56-117 CE)

Suetonius
(70-130 CE)

Scriptures
(written about 50 CE to 110 CE)

person and prophet but also fully divine? How do we come to believe that Jesus not only lived and died but was also resurrected, raised to new life? We have two sources: what Jesus said about himself and what others said and believed about Jesus.

Who Jesus says he is

Jesus himself said that he existed before Abraham (John 8:58) and that he was equal with God the Father (John 5:17-18). Jesus claimed the ability to forgive sins (Mark 2:5-7), which the Bible teaches was something that God alone could do (Isaiah 43:25). Jesus said he was one with God the Father (John 10:30) and that he was the Messiah, the Son of God (Mark 14:61-62). We cannot diminish Jesus' claims about himself. In fact, it was his very claims to be God that incited much of the outrage against him and that contributed to his arrest, trial, and crucifixion. When Jesus asked those accusing him why they wanted to stone him, they replied, "It is not for a good work that we are going to stone you, but for blasphemy, because you, though only a human being, are making yourself God" (John 10:33).

Who others say Jesus is

Those who knew Jesus, his disciples and those whom he met, had much to say about his identity. Peter was acclaimed for saying, "You are the Messiah, the Son of the Living God" (Matthew 16:16). Thomas, after asking his questions, believed and proclaimed, "My Lord and my God!" (John 20:28). Even the centurion, who did not follow Jesus but saw his crucifixion, said, "Truly this man was God's Son!" (Mark 15:39). The belief of those who walked and talked with him, who lived with him day in and day out, was that Jesus was God. That belief was so persistent that they were willing to die for it—eleven of the twelve disciples died as martyrs, as witnesses to their faith.

Those who lived after Jesus also testify to who he was. The most famous example is Paul, who did not meet Jesus while he was living but had an experience of Jesus so powerful that it was akin to a firsthand encounter (Acts 9:1-20). As a result of this mystical encounter with Jesus, Paul spent the rest of his life preaching and teaching that Jesus was the Son of God. Thirteen of the twenty-seven books of the New Testament are credited to Paul. He, like the disciples, died a martyr, willing to die for the faith he proclaimed.

Of course, evidence comes not just from people in the Bible who lived after Jesus and who have been willing to orient their entire lives around the idea that Jesus was and is God. Millions and millions of people through the ages have been so persuaded by the truth of Jesus' claims that they have called themselves Christians. Some of these Christians also have been martyrs, people who were so convinced that they were willing to die for their faith.

We have many saints whom we hold up as examples, people in whose lives the light of Christ burned brightly and through whose lives God's love was made real. Some of the saints are well-known people, from Augustine of Hippo to Teresa of Avila to Francis of Assisi, from Mother Teresa to Martin Luther King Jr. All of these people have some things in common. They wrestled with their faith, had their doubts, and yet believed. Each lived lives of extraordinary service and dedication in Jesus' name. Perhaps one of the greatest arguments for Christianity is the testimony of the saints through time, the persistence of belief in the face of overwhelming odds. What Josephus wrote 2,000 years ago is still true, "And the tribe of Christians, so named from him, are not extinct at this day."

Based on who Jesus says he is and on who others say he is, we must make a decision. C.S. Lewis in *Mere Christianity* famously said,

> I am trying here to prevent anyone saying the really foolish thing that people often say about him: I'm ready to accept Jesus as a great moral teacher, but I don't accept his claim to be God. That is the one thing we must not say. A man who was merely a man and said the sort of things Jesus said would not be a great moral teacher. He would either be a lunatic—on the level with the man who says he is a poached egg—or else

he would be the Devil of Hell. You must make your choice. Either this man was, and is, the Son of God, or else a madman or something worse. You can shut him up for a fool, you can spit at him and kill him as a demon or you can fall at his feet and call him Lord and God, but let us not come with any patronizing nonsense about his being a great human teacher. He has not left that open to us. He did not intend to.

C.S. Lewis draws our attention to a theological quandary, to a trilemma. We have to make one of three choices about Jesus. There is no other way. Three mutually exclusive options, each one difficult to accept, are put before us: Jesus is either lunatic, liar, or Lord. Jesus is either mad, bad, or good. This trilemma is the fundamental crux of our faith. This is not a question that we can avoid but one that we are forced to face and wrestle with for ourselves.

> **SUMMARY OF C. S. LEWIS'S TRILEMMA**
>
> Jesus is either lunatic, liar, or Lord.
>
> **OR**
>
> Jesus is either mad, bad, or good.

Jesus once took his followers to Caesarea Philippi, a busy trading city full of temples to various gods. There, in the midst of the strongest competition from the forces of commerce, politics, and religion, Jesus posed a question: "Who do people say that the Son of Man is?" In essence, Jesus was asking his followers to tell him to his face what others were saying about him, about who people believed him to be. His followers obliged, telling him the word on the street: some say you're John the Baptist; others call you Elijah or a prophet. But Jesus did not leave it there; he was not content merely to hear who "other people" believed him to be. Jesus asked his followers to speak for themselves. He confronted them, not with a hypothetical question, but with a deeply personal one: "Who do you say that I am?"

Peter's Declaration about Jesus
Matthew 16:13-17

Now when Jesus came into the district of Caesarea Philippi, he asked his disciples, "Who do people say that the Son of Man is?" And they said, "Some say John the Baptist, but others Elijah, and still others Jeremiah or one of the prophets." He said to them, "But who do you say that I am?" Simon Peter answered, "You are the Messiah, the Son of the living God." And Jesus answered him, "Blessed are you, Simon son of Jonah! For flesh and blood has not revealed this to you, but my Father in heaven."

You can almost hear the answers if we repeated this exercise today. If Jesus showed up in our midst and asked us: "Who do people say that Jesus is?", we might reply: "Jesus is a moral leader, a good teacher, a solid role model." But Jesus does not leave it there; he is not content merely to hear who "other people" believe him to be. We are his followers, his disciples, those who bear his name. And we, like the disciples so many years ago, are asked to claim our faith in him. It is not enough to repeat what other people have said, to proclaim what others believe. We are called to our own process of questioning and doubt and wrestling. We are called to choose an option from C.S. Lewis's trilemma: Is Jesus a lunatic, liar, or Lord? We are required to answer the question posed to each and every disciple: not "Who is Jesus?" but "Who do you say that I am?"

Are we willing to join Thomas, after offering our questions and our doubts, in belief? Are we willing to exclaim, "My Lord and my God!" as Thomas did? Are we willing to join Peter, the doubter and denier, in acclaiming, "You are the Messiah, the Son of the Living God"?

Father in heaven, who at the baptism of Jesus in the River Jordan proclaimed him your beloved Son and anointed him with the Holy Spirit: Grant that all who are baptized into his Name may keep the covenant they have made, and boldly confess him as Lord and Savior; who with you and the Holy Spirit lives and reigns, one God, in glory everlasting. Amen.

(*The Book of Common Prayer*, p. 214)

Reflection questions

❖ What do you think is the most persuasive argument for Jesus?

❖ What is your biggest doubt or question about the reality of Jesus being the Son of God?

❖ Does C.S. Lewis's trilemma help you wrestle with the question of who Jesus is? How so or why not?

❖ Before reading this chapter, how would you have answered the question, "Who is Jesus?"

❖ How do you answer the question, "Who do you say that I am?"

3

WHY DID JESUS HAVE TO DIE?

Lord Jesus Christ, Son of the living God, we pray you to set your passion, cross, and death between your judgment and our souls, now and in the hour of our death. Give mercy and grace to the living; pardon and rest to the dead; to your holy Church peace and concord; and to us sinners everlasting life and glory; for with the Father and the Holy Spirit you live and reign, one God, now and for ever. Amen.

(*The Book of Common Prayer*, p. 282)

Not long ago, I was reading a Christmas story to a friend's four-year-old daughter. Things seemed to be going pretty well, and both of us were enjoying the time together. And then, out of nowhere, she asked a question. "Why did Jesus have to die?" Right there, as we were reading about angels and a manger, she brought me up short. There simply isn't an easy answer to this question people have been asking for twenty centuries. "Why did Jesus have to die?"

I've been to seminary, but that doesn't make the question easy to answer. I've studied the scriptures, and I've read what others have pondered for centuries. While it's tempting to reduce the answer to a bumper sticker or a tweet, the reality is that one could easily spend a lifetime on just this question. "Why did Jesus have to die?"

There is a whole branch of theology devoted to this question. Atonement theory tries to help us understand the brutal reality that God died on a cross, the death of an ordinary criminal.

We spend a lot of time talking about how Jesus lived—what he said, what he taught, how he interacted with people. Most of the stories we hear about Jesus in the gospels are about his life. And of course, Jesus' life and ministry are an important part of our faith. Yet it is Jesus' death and resurrection that are central—most important—to the Christian narrative.

Consider this:

❖ **It is the cross that is the symbol of our faith.** The cross is what you see on top of or inside every church and what people wear around their necks. The cross, the instrument of Jesus' death, is the identifying mark of Christians.

❖ **The story of Jesus' death is central to the Bible.** The narrative of Jesus' death takes up more than a quarter of each of the four gospels, and it is one of the few things recorded in all four gospels.

❖ **Jesus' death also dominates his life.** Jesus himself talks about his death early in his ministry (Mark 8:31-33), and he references it throughout his teaching and preaching (Mark 9:30-32, Matthew 16:21-28, John 12:7-8, and Luke 18:31-34).

The rest of the New Testament centers around Jesus' death and resurrection. The scriptures in the New Testament tell us again and again of the importance of Jesus' death for us. It is something that we proclaim in our creeds and in our prayers. Jesus' life is important, certainly, but his death is the central, transformative tenet of our faith. As Christians, we understand that Jesus' death teaches us something about God and that it accomplishes something for us and for the world.

So why is Jesus' death so important for us Christians? The Bible and Christian tradition have used many different images and metaphors for understanding Jesus' death and for explaining both why it is so important and what it accomplishes. Jesus' death:

❖ **redeems or ransoms us from slavery.** All of us, through our wrong choices, have sold ourselves as slaves to sin and death. Jesus gives himself over to the power of sin and death, taking our place. He exchanges himself for us, redeeming us and setting us free, so that death no longer has power over us. (Galatians 4:4-7, Matthew 20:28)

❖ **satisfies or pays our debt**. Through our shady dealings (that is, through sin) we have accumulated a debt to evil and owe as payment our death. Jesus pays that debt with his life, so that we no longer owe anything. (Romans 6:23)

❖ **atones for our guilt**. We have sinned, have done bad things, both as individuals and communally. There are consequences for bad actions; the system of justice that governs all creation requires that someone must be punished for the wrongs that have been done. Jesus, in his suffering and death, is punished instead of us, taking on our guilt, so that we no longer have to bear the punishment. (substitutionary penal atonement, Isaiah 53:5, 1 Peter 2:24)

❖ **cleanses our sin**. The sin of our lives and of the world is like dirt—we are tarnished, unclean. God is so good and perfect that nothing unclean could stand to be near God. Jesus' death washes us clean, rinsing off the effects of sin so that we are made worthy to stand before God. (Hebrews 9:14)

Fundamental to all these metaphors is the idea that Jesus saves us. Jesus saves us from evil, from the powers of this world

> Jesus' death accomplishes our salvation.

that seek to corrupt and destroy. These evil powers tell us lies about who we are and what we can or should do. Jesus saves us from ourselves, from believing that there is something we can or should do to earn God's love or to make ourselves right with God. Jesus shows us grace; he shows us that God loves us no matter what.

We say that Jesus died to cleanse us from our sins. Died to save us from death. Died to set us free from evil. All of these different understandings, these different metaphors for Jesus' death, teach us about atonement— what happens when Jesus dies and how Jesus saves us. Why is Jesus' death, as much as or perhaps more so than his life, so central to our faith? Because while his life gave us lessons to learn, a pattern to follow, and the reassurance of God's solidarity and presence among us, Jesus' death accomplishes our salvation.

Yet when we ask, "Why did Jesus have to die?" we are asking the wrong question (or at least not the best question). Because asking the question in that way assumes that there was a necessity to Jesus' death. That God demanded it, that the system of justice required it, that death was the inevitable end to the story of salvation. But that's not exactly how the Bible tells it.

Instead, scripture is clear that God chose to become human (incarnate, literally "enfleshed") in Jesus. Jesus himself chose to die. In John 10:17-18, Jesus says,

> For this reason the Father loves me, because I lay down my life in order to take it up again. No one takes it from me, but I lay it down of my own accord. I have power to lay it down, and I have power to take it up again. I have received this command from my Father.

In the Gospel according to Matthew, in the midst of the swirling drama that leads to Jesus' death, we read this:

> Then Jesus said to him, "Put your sword back into its place; for all who take the sword will perish by the sword. Do you think that I cannot appeal to my Father, and he will at once send me more than twelve legions of angels? But how then would the scriptures be fulfilled, which say it must happen in this way?" At that hour Jesus said to the crowds,

"Have you come out with swords and clubs to arrest me as though I were a bandit? Day after day I sat in the temple teaching, and you did not arrest me. But all this has taken place, so that the scriptures of the prophets may be fulfilled." Then all the disciples deserted him and fled. (26: 52-56)

These scriptures and many others reveal that Jesus didn't have to die at all; Jesus chose to die. And we are left to wonder why. The answer is both shockingly simple and infinitely complex: Love. Jesus chose to die because of his great love for us. In John 15:12-13, Jesus says, "This is my commandment, that you love one another as I have loved you. No one has greater love than this, to lay down one's life for one's friends." To put it another way, "God's love was revealed among us in this way: God sent his only Son into the world so that we might live through him. In this is love, not that we loved God but that he loved us and sent his Son to be the atoning sacrifice for our sins" (1 John 4:9-10).

So our question becomes not "Why did Jesus have to die?" but "Why did Jesus choose to die?" This way of asking the question

> Jesus chose to die because of his great love for us.

changes the conversation completely. The emphasis then is not on what we've done wrong—our sin, our debt, our guilt—but on what God in Jesus Christ has done right—God's overwhelming, redemptive love. Salvation becomes not a problem to be solved but rather a gift to be received.

Jesus chose to die for love of us and all creation. Because God's love is stronger than death, we know that we are never, ever alone in this life or the next. Romans sets this out beautifully, in one of the loveliest passages of scripture.

> What then are we to say about these things? If God is for us, who is against us? He who did not withhold his own Son, but gave him up for all of us, will he not with him also give us everything else? Who will bring any charge against God's elect? It is God who justifies. Who is to condemn? It is Christ Jesus, who died, yes, who was raised, who is at the right hand of God, who indeed intercedes for us. Who will separate us from the love of Christ? Will hardship, or distress, or persecution, or famine, or nakedness, or peril, or sword? As it is written, "For your sake we are being killed all day long; we are accounted as sheep to be slaughtered."
>
> No, in all these things we are more than conquerors through him who loved us. For I am convinced that neither death, nor life, nor angels, nor rulers, nor things present, nor things to come, nor powers, nor height, nor depth, nor anything

else in all creation, will be able to separate us from the love of God in Christ Jesus our Lord. (8:31-39)

Jesus' death shows us that as frightening and intimidating as the powers of evil, sin, and darkness are, God's love is a much stronger force. From Ephesians 1:17-21,

> I pray that the God of our Lord Jesus Christ, the Father of glory, may give you a spirit of wisdom and revelation as you come to know him, so that, with the eyes of your heart enlightened, you may know what is the hope to which he has called you, what are the riches of his glorious inheritance among the saints, and what is the immeasurable greatness of his power for us who believe, according to the working of his great power. God put this power to work in Christ when he raised him from the dead and seated him at his right hand in the heavenly places, far above all rule and authority and power and dominion, and above every name that is named, not only in this age but also in the age to come.

Jesus' death proves to us that evil and death are never the end of the story; they do not have the last word. Jesus, the Word Incarnate, through his life, death, and resurrection, gives us the story—his story, the world's story, our story—which is both a new ending and a new beginning.

Perhaps the greatest reflection on atonement, on Jesus' choice to die and what happens for us and for the world as a result of Jesus' death, comes from the ancient Easter sermon preached by John Chrysostom some 1,600 years ago. To this day, his sermon is read during Easter services at Eastern Orthodox congregations and in some Episcopal congregations. It speaks with resounding clarity about the power of God in Jesus Christ to conquer death and sin.

Are there any who are devout lovers of God?
Let them enjoy this beautiful bright festival!

Are there any who are grateful servants?
Let them rejoice and enter into the joy of their Lord!

Are there any weary from fasting?
Let them now receive their due!

If any have toiled from the first hour, let them receive their reward. If any have come after the third hour, let them with gratitude join in the feast! Those who arrived after the sixth hour, let them not doubt; for they shall not be shortchanged. Those who have tarried until the ninth hour, let them not hesitate; but let them come too. And those who arrived only at the eleventh hour, let them not be afraid by reason of their delay. For the Lord is gracious and receives the last even as the first. The Lord gives rest to those who come at the eleventh hour, even as to those who toiled from the beginning.

To one and all the Lord gives generously. The Lord accepts the offering of every work. The Lord honors every deed and commends their intention. Let us all enter into the joy of the Lord!

First and last alike, receive your reward. Rich and poor, rejoice together! Conscientious and lazy, celebrate the day!

You who have kept the fast, and you who have not, rejoice, this day, for the table is bountifully spread! Feast royally, for the calf is fatted. Let no one go away hungry. Partake, all, of the banquet of faith.

Enjoy the bounty of the Lord's goodness!

Let no one grieve being poor, for the universal reign has been revealed.

Let no one lament persistent failings, for forgiveness has risen from the grave.

Let no one fear death, for the death of our Savior has set us free.

The Lord has destroyed death by enduring it.
The Lord vanquished hell when he descended
into it.

The Lord put hell in turmoil even as it tasted
of his flesh. Isaiah foretold this when he said,
"You, O Hell, were placed in turmoil when he
encountering you below."

Hell was in turmoil having been eclipsed.
Hell was in turmoil having been mocked.

Hell was in turmoil having been destroyed.
Hell was in turmoil having been abolished.

Hell was in turmoil having been made captive.
Hell grasped a corpse, and met God.

Hell seized earth, and encountered heaven.
Hell took what it saw, and was overcome by what
it could not see.

O death, where is your sting?
O hell, where is your victory?

Christ is risen, and you are cast down!
Christ is risen, and the demons are fallen!

Christ is risen, and the angels rejoice!
Christ is risen, and life is set free!

Christ is risen, and the tomb is emptied of its dead.

For Christ, having risen from the dead, is become the first-fruits of those who have fallen asleep.

To Christ be glory and power forever and ever. Amen!

As we reflect not on why Jesus had to die but instead on why Jesus chose to die, our focus shifts: from ourselves to God, from sin to love, from the circumstances of Christ's death to the consequences of his death and resurrection for us and for all of creation. Jesus chose to die, to lay down his life, to stretch out his arms of love. When we begin to realize and embrace that Jesus chose to die for love of us, our guiding question changes yet again, and we begin to ask ourselves: Knowing that Jesus chose to die for love of us, how are we called to live, for love of him?

Lord Jesus Christ, you stretched out your arms of love on the hard wood of the cross that everyone might come within the reach of your saving embrace: So clothe us in your Spirit that we, reaching forth our hands in love, may bring those who do not know you to the knowledge and love of you; for the honor of your Name. Amen.

(*The Book of Common Prayer*, p. 101)

Reflection questions

❖ Before you read this chapter, how would you have answered the question, "Why did Jesus have to die?"

❖ Does it change the way you think about Jesus' death if you ask "Why did Jesus choose to die?" instead of "Why did Jesus have to die?" If so, how?

❖ Which of the metaphors about Jesus' death is most helpful to you? Why?

❖ Which of the metaphors about Jesus' death is most difficult for you? Why?

❖ Knowing that Jesus chose to die, for love of you, how are you feeling called to live, for love of him?

WHAT DO I
HAVE TO DO?

Almighty God our heavenly Father, you declare your glory and show forth your handiwork in the heavens and in the earth: Deliver us in our various occupations from the service of self alone, that we may do the work you give us to do in truth and beauty and for the common good; for the sake of him who came among us as one who serves, your Son Jesus Christ our Lord, who lives and reigns with you and the Holy Spirit, one God, for ever and ever. Amen.

(*The Book of Common Prayer*, p. 261)

In the last chapter, we learned about the amazing good news that Jesus chose to die for love of us. This way of looking at things, of seeing that Jesus didn't have to die, but chose to die, invites a response from us: knowing that Jesus chose to die for love of us, how are we called to live, for love of him?

In fact, a lot of people think of Christianity predominantly or exclusively as a system for living.

❖ Most of the families that I speak to about baptism want to bring their children up in the church so that they will "learn to be good people" or learn "values."

❖ Many people equate Christianity with a list of "to dos," behaviors or actions that are either required or prohibited.

❖ Shortly after hearing about Jesus, people typically start asking, "What do I have to do to be a Christian?"

The answers are both straightforward and complex. When thinking of a list of behaviors or guidelines for living, the first thing that comes to mind for many is the Ten Commandments.

The Ten Commandments
Exodus 20:1-17

Then God spoke all these words:

I am the LORD your God, who brought you out of the land of Egypt, out of the house of slavery; you shall have no other gods before me.

You shall not make for yourself an idol, whether in the form of anything that is in heaven above, or that is on the earth beneath, or that is in the water under the earth. You shall not bow down to them or worship them; for I the LORD your God am a jealous God, punishing children for the iniquity of parents, to the third and the fourth generation of those who reject me, but showing steadfast love to the thousandth generation of those who love me and keep my commandments.

You shall not make wrongful use of the name of the LORD your God, for the LORD will not acquit anyone who misuses his name.

Remember the sabbath day, and keep it holy. Six days you shall labor and do all your work. But the seventh day is a sabbath to the LORD your God; you shall not do any work—you, your son or your daughter, your male or female slave, your livestock, or the alien resident in your towns. For in six days the LORD made heaven and earth, the sea, and all that is in them, but rested the seventh day; therefore the LORD blessed the sabbath day and consecrated it.

Honor your father and your mother, so that your days may be long in the land that the LORD your God is giving you.

You shall not murder.

You shall not commit adultery.

You shall not steal.

You shall not bear false witness against your neighbor.

You shall not covet your neighbor's house; you shall not covet your neighbor's wife, or male or female slave, or ox, or donkey, or anything that belongs to your neighbor.

This famous list of "thou shalts" (or "you shalls") and "thou shalt nots" (or "you shall nots") seems like a great starting place for what it looks like to be a Christian, or at the very least, a moral person. It tells us things we should do and things we should not do. It helps us know how to act toward God and toward one another. Of course, this list isn't just for Christians. It's found in what

Christians call the Old Testament and what Jews call the Torah. These commandments are central to Jewish life and faith. It's important for us to notice that the Ten Commandments cover some of the most vital parts of human life, but the list doesn't cover a lot of what we need to know in order to be morally good humans. There is still a lot of gray area, a lot of things unaddressed or unspoken. The Ten Commandments are important, but they are not exhaustive.

Jesus himself reiterates the importance of the Ten Commandments, but he says they're not enough.

The Rich Young Man
Matthew 19:16-21

Then someone came to him and said, "Teacher, what good deed must I do to have eternal life?" And he said to him, "Why do you ask me about what is good? There is only one who is good. If you wish to enter into life, keep the commandments." He said to him, "Which ones?" And Jesus said, "You shall not murder; You shall not commit adultery; You shall not steal; You shall not bear false witness; Honor your father and mother; also, You shall love your neighbor as yourself." The young man said to him, "I have kept all these; what do I still lack?" Jesus said to him, "If you wish to be perfect, go, sell your possessions, and give the money to the poor, and you will have treasure in heaven; then come, follow me."

This is a bit intimidating. If we're honest, it's not easy to keep all of the basic Ten Commandments. After all, who has never lied? And while we may not have wished we could have our neighbor's donkey, who among us has never looked longingly at someone's new car, phone, purse, or clothes? Still, keeping these commandments isn't enough! Faithful people, Jesus says, have to do even more.

Jesus speaks a few times about what this "even more" looks like.

The Greatest Commandment
Matthew 22:34-40

When the Pharisees heard that he had silenced the Sadducees, they gathered together, and one of them, a lawyer, asked him a question to test him. "Teacher, which commandment in the law is the greatest?" He said to him, "'You shall love the Lord your God with all your heart, and with all your soul, and with all your mind.' This is the greatest and first commandment. And a second is like it: 'You shall love your neighbor as yourself.' On these two commandments hang all the law and the prophets."

When asked to name the greatest commandment, Jesus gives what would have been a shocking answer in his day. He doesn't list the Ten Commandments or one of the "usual suspects" but instead offers two different commandments, one from Deuteronomy (6:5) and one from Leviticus (19:18). Here we have just two commandments, but they are so broad, so all-encompassing, that they require our whole lives, our whole being, to fulfill them.

Keeping these commandments isn't enough! Faithful people, Jesus says, have to do even more.

As an aside, next time someone tells you they like the New Testament God more than the Old Testament God, you can say two things to them. First, Christians decided almost 1,800 years ago that this is heresy: Christians believe in one God, who speaks through all time and all places—and that God is revealed in both the Old Testament and the New Testament. Second, most of the stuff people like from the New Testament is, in fact, quoted from the Old Testament. Leviticus—everyone's favorite book to hate, even though they haven't read it— is the source of several of Jesus' sayings.

Back to our topic. Not only does Jesus offer the Great Commandment (love God, love neighbor) in response to a question, but he offers another new commandment to his followers. On the night before he dies, Jesus spends much of the evening teaching his followers and praying

> The love that Jesus asks of us demands our full effort.

with them. Chief among his teaching that night is a new commandment: "I give you a new commandment, that you love one another. Just as I have loved you, you also should love one another. By this everyone will know that you are my disciples, if you have love for one another" (John 13:34-35).

That's not so bad, right? Just one commandment! This new commandment sounds easy, but it is incredibly hard. After all, Jesus showed his love for us by giving up everything, including his very life. This love isn't a sentiment, the sort of thing you see on a greeting card or on a heartwarming TV show. No, the love that Jesus asks of us demands our full effort.

At this point, if we're paying attention, we start to panic. We are called to love God with all our heart and soul and mind and strength. We're called to love God more than our country, our family, our job, or our own life. Then we are called to love other people as much as we love ourselves—and to love ourselves as much as we love other people. And not only that, we have to love others with the same depth and breadth of Jesus' own love for his followers?! Jesus, who loved us enough to come into our world in complete humility, to live as we do, to suffer an agonizing death...

What does it actually look like to love one another as Christ loved us?

WHAT DO I HAVE TO DO?

GULP.

Once we've absorbed the fact that the call to follow Jesus is going to be much harder than we might have imagined, it's natural for us to wonder what's next. What, exactly, does loving one another this way look like? How does this Christian love get lived out in practice? What does loving God look like:

— when I'm stuck in traffic or in the checkout lane?

— when I'm in the voting booth or on the soccer field?

— when I'm attending church and when I'm not?

— when I'm with family and when I'm with strangers?

What does it actually mean to love God with all my heart and mind and soul and strength—and love my neighbor as myself? What does it actually look like to love one another as Christ loved us?

Christians have been wrestling with these questions throughout the centuries, since Jesus first gave those commands to his disciples. Though it might be easier if we had a six-point plan for Christian living, God didn't exactly give us one. God gave us the Bible for guidance about what faithful living does and doesn't look like. God gave us one another, to learn from and with. Most of all, God sent us Jesus, a living example of God's love—the "image of the invisible God" (Colossians 1:15).

In The Episcopal Church, our liturgy proclaims what we

BAPTISMAL PROMISES

- Will you continue in the apostles' teaching and fellowship, in the breaking of bread, and in the prayers?

- Will you persevere in resisting evil, and, whenever you fall into sin, repent and return to the Lord?

- Will you proclaim by word and example the Good News of God in Christ?

- Will you seek and serve Christ in all persons, loving your neighbor as yourself?

- Will you strive for justice and peace among all people, and respect the dignity of every human being?

believe our life of love should look like. The Baptismal Covenant includes a series of questions that all candidates for baptism or their sponsors answer in the service for Holy Baptism, and they are questions that all of us answer on occasions when we reaffirm our baptismal promises (*The Book of Common Prayer*, pp. 304-305).

These five promises summarize what we, as Episcopalians and as Christians, are called to do and how we are called to live.

❖ **We are called to continue in the apostles' teaching and fellowship, in the breaking of bread, and in the prayers.** In practice, this means we are called to participate in Christian worship, to attend classes to learn about our faith, to join in the celebration of Holy Eucharist, and to pray, both as a community and as individuals. To live this out, we need to put worshiping with a Christian community at the top of our list, not as a do-it-when-I-feel-like-it activity.

❖ **We are called to persevere in resisting evil, and, whenever we fall into sin, repent and return to the Lord.** In practice, this looks like actively turning away from those things that we know to be evil, even if they are alluring, and being ready when we sin (not if, but when—whenever, every time) to do what is necessary to be reconciled with God and with one another.

❖ **We are called to proclaim by word and example the Good News of God in Christ.** In practice, this means sharing our faith, sharing the gospel, sharing the message of Jesus with anyone and everyone. Sharing it with words and with example—not one or the other. This one might be the hardest for Episcopalians: we have to talk about our faith with strangers!

❖ **We are called to seek and serve Christ in all persons, loving our neighbor as ourselves.** In practice, this takes on a great diversity of forms and requires a great deal of effort on our part. We can't wait for others to show us the face of Jesus; we have to seek it in them. We must serve others, whether we feel like it or not, as though they were Christ himself.

❖ **We are called to strive for justice and peace among all people and respect the dignity of every human being.** In practice, this means we can't just wait for God's justice and peace to come or ask other people to make it happen, but we must work for it ourselves. And we must respect every human being, whether they look like us or not, whether we agree with them or not, whether we think they deserve it or not.

This is, according to our tradition, the shape of the Christian life. This is what it looks like when we take seriously Jesus' command to love one another as he has loved us. It's something far more comprehensive and demanding than just refraining from murder and theft (though that's a good start!). This is how our Church has answered the question, "knowing that Jesus chose to die for love of us, how are we called to live, for love of him?"

It would be easy to hear all this and to give up. It would be easy to want to quit because it seems too demanding.

Pastor and evangelist Brian McLaren tells this story of a woman who comes to a priest, asking him to un-baptize her.

"Please de-baptize me," she said. The priest's face crumpled. "My parents tell me you did it," she said. "But I was not consulted. So now, undo it." The priest asked why. "If it were just about belonging to this religion and being forgiven, then I would stay. If it were just about believing this list of doctrines and upholding this list of rituals, I'd be OK. But your sermon Sunday made it clear it's about more. More than I bargained for. So, please, de-baptize me." The priest looked down, said nothing. She continued: "You said baptism sends me into the world to love enemies. I don't. Nor do I plan to. You said it means being willing to stand against the flow. I like the flow. You described it like rethinking everything, like joining a movement. But I'm not rethinking or moving anywhere. So un-baptize me.

Please." The priest began to weep. Soon great sobs rose from his deepest heart. He took off his glasses, blew his nose, took three tissues to dry his eyes. "These are tears of joy," he said. "I think you are the first person who ever truly listened or understood." "So," she said, "Will you? Please?"

This story captures the truth that the Christian life is serious; it is more difficult and demanding than many of us like to believe. And, of course, if all of this were up to us, to our own abilities, it would be overwhelming and hopeless. It would be far beyond anything we could expect or hope to accomplish. In fact, it would be impossible. If we set ourselves up believing that the Ten Commandments or the Great Commandment or the baptismal promises or any other list of Christian duties or responsibilities are what we should do, or must do, in response to God, then we are setting ourselves up for failure.

> Jesus never says following him is going to be easy. Quite the opposite, in fact!

At the same time, we need to realize that Jesus never says following him is going to be easy. Quite the opposite, in fact. Take up your cross! Sell all that you have! Leave your family behind! How this is lived out will vary, of course. One of my favorite sayings is, "If you think it's easy to be a Christian, you're doing it wrong."

The flip side of it is that when we get it right—when we manage to live the abundant life overflowing with God's love that Jesus hopes for us—we experience mind-boggling joy. In fact, in this earthly life, the only true and lasting joy comes in following Jesus—and doing that will take us far outside our comfort zone. It means being really committed to worship. It means serving the poor and others at the margins. It means giving away much of what we might think is ours—the tithe of 10 percent is really a minimum. We are asked to do a lot, but in doing so, we are given a lot.

We can't do it on our own. We need a community, and we especially need God. A key part of our baptismal promises that is far too often overlooked is the response: "I will, with God's help."

❖ These are not things that we promise to do for God; they are things that we promise to let God do with and through and in us.

❖ The promises of the Baptismal Covenant are not duties or demands; they are promises. They are promises that we make to God and promises that God makes to us.

In baptism, we are sealed by the Holy Spirit and marked as Christ's own forever. As Christians, we do not engage in the practices of our faith alone but are fueled by and filled with the very power of God, the Holy Spirit living and working in us.

❖ When he dies, Jesus promises that he will not leave his followers, that he will not leave us, alone. (John 14:15-20)

❖ The Holy Spirit fills the community of believers and empowers them to do all sorts of wonderful things (Acts 2:1-47)

❖ That same Spirit is what abides in us and allows us to fulfill the promises of our baptism. (Ephesians 3:14-20)

The promises that we make to God in baptism are impossible promises—if they rely on our own strength, power, and dedication. But the promise that God makes to us in baptism is that we don't have to rely on our own strength, power, and dedication; God's presence and power is with us always, and God can work in and through us to do infinitely more than we could ask or imagine.

Knowing that the presence and power of the Holy Spirit is with us, assured that all the promises of baptism are not something that we must do with our own strength but something that we get to do "with God's help," our questions and perspectives change.

"What do I have to do for God?" becomes "What can I do with God in me?"

"How should I now live" is instead "How can I now live?"

"What do I have to do?" becomes "What can I do, with God's help?"

Almighty and most merciful God, grant that by the indwelling of your Holy Spirit we may be enlightened and strengthened for your service; through Jesus Christ our Lord, who lives and reigns with you, in the unity of the Holy Spirit, one God, now and for ever. Amen.

(*The Book of Common Prayer*, p. 251)

Reflection questions

❖ When you hear the question, "What do Christians have to do?" what things come to mind?

❖ Which baptismal promise resonates the most with you and why?

❖ Which baptismal promise is the most difficult for you and why?

❖ Do you ever do difficult things because of your faith? What is that experience like?

❖ How might it change the practice of your faith to focus on the power of God within you?

5

HOW SHOULD I READ THE BIBLE?

Blessed Lord, who caused all holy Scriptures to be written for our learning: Grant us so to hear them, read, mark, learn, and inwardly digest them, that we may embrace and ever hold fast the blessed hope of everlasting life, which you have given us in our Savior Jesus Christ; who lives and reigns with you and the Holy Spirit, one God, for ever and ever. Amen.

(*The Book of Common Prayer*, p. 236)

Most people would say the Bible is a pretty important book. The average American household has about five Bibles. The Bible is the bestselling book of all time, and it probably would top bestseller lists every week if it were included in the figures. With all those Bibles in our houses, you would think that we know what it says. But though 88 percent of Americans own a Bible, only 37 percent read the Bible regularly, according to the American Bible Society. And biblical literacy among Americans is shockingly low.

AMERICANS AND THE BIBLE

- Only half of American adults can name even one of the four gospels.

- Most Americans cannot name the first book of the Bible.

- A majority of Americans wrongly believe the Bible says that Jesus was born in Jerusalem.

- Ten percent of Americans believe that Joan of Arc was Noah's wife.

Source: www.beliefnet.com

Though we have Bibles, many of us don't read them. Why? Of course there are the usual reasons. We are busy; we don't have time to read much of anything. Reading the Bible is something for priests to do, or at least some other kinds of Christians. I learned the Bible stories in Sunday school, and I hear them in church so I don't need to read the Bible. For many of us, these are just excuses. The real reason we don't read the Bible more is that we're intimidated. We know that we should read the Bible (that's why we have so many of them!), but we don't know how to read the Bible.

In order to understand how to read the Bible, we first have to understand what the Bible is and what the Bible isn't.

There are a number of different images or metaphors that people use (either explicitly or implicitly) for understanding the Bible.

❖ **Rule book.** People who understand the Bible as a rule book often focus on the thou shalts and thou shalt nots. This understanding sees the Bible as a list of hard and fast rules to follow.

❖ **Operating instructions or manual for life.** Others see the Bible, not quite as a book of rules, but as a manual for life, kind of like an ancient self-help tome. There are lots of everyday, nitty-gritty topics that the Bible talks about and gives advice on: How should I relate to the people around me? How do I honor my mother and father, reconcile with my brother, love my wife, etc.? What does God want from me? In this understanding, the Bible becomes the answer book that you go to every time you have a question.

❖ **Devotional or inspirational guide.** For some, the Bible is primarily a place to find comfort or inspiration. In this approach, the words of the Bible are seen not as guidelines so much as sage words of advice to help me feel better. Reading the Bible in this way focuses on the stories of other people who have struggled and have made it through.

❖ **Love story.** Many also see the Bible as God's love letter to humanity. The Bible tells the story (the ups and downs and the ins and outs) of the tumultuous relationship between God and God's people. In this view, the Bible is intimate; it functions not only as God's love story to humanity but also specifically to me.

The truth is: the Bible is all those things (and more)!

The Bible is a library or collection of books. The sixty-six different books that make up the Old and New Testaments of the Bible were written by different people in different places in different times (and even in different languages). Some books are in Hebrew, some books in Greek, and there's even a smattering of Aramaic. Some books (like the Psalms and Isaiah) are poetry, and others are prose. Some books are first-person accounts, and some are third-person narratives.

> The Bible is a library or collection of books.

The Bible is not even all one "kind" of writing; it has many different genres.

Historical narrative

In the fifth year of King Rehoboam, King Shishak of Egypt came up against Jerusalem; he took away the treasures of the house of the LORD and the treasures of the king's house; he took everything. He also took away all the shields of gold that Solomon had made; so King Rehoboam made shields of bronze instead, and committed them to the hands of the officers of the guard, who kept the door of the king's house. As often as the king went into the house of the LORD, the guard carried them and brought them back to the guardroom. Now the rest of the acts of Rehoboam, and all that he did, are they not written in the Book of the Annals of the Kings of Judah? There was war between Rehoboam and Jeroboam continually. Rehoboam slept with his ancestors and was buried with his ancestors in the city of David. His mother's name was Naamah the Ammonite. His son Abijam succeeded him. (1 Kings 14:25-31)

Law

When an ox gores a man or a woman to death, the ox shall be stoned, and its flesh shall not be eaten; but the owner of the ox shall not be liable.

If the ox has been accustomed to gore in the past, and its owner has been warned but has not restrained it, and it kills a man or a woman, the ox shall be stoned, and its owner also shall be put to death. If a ransom is imposed on the owner, then the owner shall pay whatever is imposed for the redemption of the victim's life. If it gores a boy or a girl, the owner shall be dealt with according to this same rule. If the ox gores a male or female slave, the owner shall pay to the slaveowner thirty shekels of silver, and the ox shall be stoned. (Exodus 21:28-32)

Poetry

As a deer longs for flowing streams,
   so my soul longs for you, O God.

My soul thirsts for God,
   for the living God.

When shall I come and behold
   the face of God?

My tears have been my food
   day and night,

while people say to me continually,
   "Where is your God?"

These things I remember,
   as I pour out my soul:

how I went with the throng,
   and led them in procession to
   the house of God,

with glad shouts and songs of thanksgiving,
   a multitude keeping festival.

Why are you cast down, O my soul,
   and why are you disquieted within me?

Hope in God; for I shall again praise him,
   my help and my God. (Psalm 42:1-6a)

Prophecy

In days to come
   the mountain of the LORD's house

shall be established as the highest of the
mountains,
   and shall be raised above the hills;

all the nations shall stream to it.

Many peoples shall come and say,

"Come, let us go up to the mountain of the LORD,
   to the house of the God of Jacob;

that he may teach us his ways
and that we may walk in his paths."

For out of Zion shall go forth instruction,
and the word of the Lord from Jerusalem.

He shall judge between the nations,
and shall arbitrate for many peoples;

they shall beat their swords into plowshares,
and their spears into pruning hooks;

nation shall not lift up sword against nation,
neither shall they learn war any more.

(Isaiah 2:2-4)

Narrative

As he walked by the Sea of Galilee, he saw two brothers, Simon, who is called Peter, and Andrew his brother, casting a net into the sea—for they were fishermen. And he said to them, "Follow me, and I will make you fish for people." Immediately they left their nets and followed him. As he went from there, he saw two other brothers, James son of Zebedee and his brother John, in the boat with their father Zebedee, mending their nets, and he called them. Immediately they left the boat and their father, and followed him. (Matthew 4:18-22)

Letters or Epistle

Give my greetings to the brothers and sisters in Laodicea, and to Nympha and the church in her house. And when this letter has been read among you, have it read also in the church of the Laodiceans; and see that you read also the letter from Laodicea. And say to Archippus, "See that you complete the task that you have received in the Lord." I, Paul, write this greeting with my own hand. Remember my chains. Grace be with you. (Colossians 4:15-18)

Apocalyptic

Then I saw the Lamb open one of the seven seals, and I heard one of the four living creatures call out, as with a voice of thunder, "Come!" I looked, and there was a white horse! Its rider had a bow; a crown was given to him, and he came out conquering and to conquer. When he opened the second seal, I heard the second living creature call out, "Come!" And out came another horse, bright red; its rider was permitted to take peace from the earth, so that people would slaughter one another; and he was given a great sword. When he opened the third seal, I heard the third living creature call out, "Come!" I looked, and there was a black horse! Its rider held a pair of scales in his hand, and I heard what seemed to be a voice in the midst of the four living creatures saying, "A quart of wheat for a day's pay, and three quarts of barley for a day's pay, but do not damage the olive oil and the wine!" When he opened the fourth seal, I heard the voice of the fourth living creature call out, "Come!" I looked and there was a pale green horse! Its rider's name was Death, and Hades followed with him; they were given authority over a fourth of the earth, to kill with sword, famine, and pestilence, and by the wild animals of the earth. (Revelation 6:1-8)

It is important to understand that the Bible contains all these different things, so that we stop trying to read the Bible as only one thing. If we read the laws as though they are prophecy, we will be

> We have to encounter each part of the Bible on its own terms in order to better understand the whole.

confused. If we read the poetry as though it is law, we will be confused. If we read the letters as though they are narrative, we will be confused. We have to encounter each part of the Bible on its own terms in order to better understand the whole.

Yet, in spite of its diversity, we understand that the Bible also has a unity. The diversity of the Bible reminds us that God can and does speak to people in many different ways. The common denominator in the Bible is not the form of speech but the inspiration of the speaker (or writer). We believe that all those different people in different times and different places who spoke different languages and wrote in different genres were inspired to speak by God. As our *Book of Common Prayer* says, "We call [the Holy Scriptures] the Word of God because God inspired their human authors and because God still speaks to us through the Bible" (p. 853). So we understand the books of the Bible to be written by humans, but we believe the humans who wrote the Bible were all inspired by God. We also believe that God still speaks through them to us today.

So, do we take every word literally? No one takes every word of scripture literally. Ask a so-called literalist if the Savior of the world is a baguette, because in John 6:35, Jesus said, "I am the bread of life." Obviously, Jesus didn't mean that literally. He meant us to hear these words as a gripping image. There are no literalists of the scriptures, but there are people who are not honest in admitting that we all interpret the scriptures through our own lens. We have to interpret the scriptures because the texts themselves demand it. It is in our relationship with the scriptures that we begin to see what is metaphor and what is description, what is imagery and what is command.

Sometimes two stories are told differently—and may even have contradictions. Consider the famous story of Noah loading up the animals on the ark, two-by-two. The story is told in Genesis 6: 19-20, "And of every living thing, of all flesh, you shall bring two of every kind into the ark, to keep them alive with you; they shall be male and female. Of the birds according to their kinds, and of the animals according to their kinds, of every creeping thing of the ground according to its kind, two of every kind shall come in to you, to keep them alive." Wait a minute, what's happening over in Genesis 7:2-3? "Take with you seven pairs of all clean animals, the male and its mate; and a pair of the animals that are not clean, the male and its mate; and seven pairs of the birds of the air also, male and female, to keep their kind alive on the face of all the earth." While the details differ, both accounts of the great flood in Genesis tell the story we need to hear of God's covenant with humanity. Both talk of God specifically saving sets of all the animals so that creation will continue.

Sometimes there are things that are clearly meant as metaphors. For example, in Matthew 5:13, Jesus says that we are the salt of the earth. We know that he doesn't mean we are literally salt! But we learn that we are supposed to understand ourselves in a new way in light of that metaphor.

And the Bible is filled with humor. The whole book of Jonah is hilarious (go read it now: it's just three pages long, and then you can say you read an entire book of the Old Testament).

Jesus' comment about camels fitting through the eye of a needle is meant to make us think and probably even laugh (Matthew 19:24).

So if the Bible is not meant to be read literally, then we are left with a question. Is the Bible "true"? Truth is not the same as literal fact. In fact, sometimes truth is much deeper than fact. Have you ever heard a poem or song that encapsulated a truth more deeply than an encyclopedia or dissertation? A poem about a rose may well convey its wonders more fully than a Wikipedia article.

Or consider an encounter with a Monet painting in an art gallery. A scientist could tell us about the kinds of pigments used, about the exact depth of the paint, and the date the canvas was made. But true facts wouldn't help us understand what the painting is about. To really understand the Monet, you have to go to the gallery, stand back a bit, and gaze at the painting. Then you can begin to see the power and beauty of Monet's work. That is the truth of the painting. The facts help too, but deeper truth is about meaning.

We Christians absolutely believe the Bible is true. We believe it contains both facts and metaphors, all of which are true. We believe the Bible both reflects and conveys a deeper truth—the truth of God's power and presence and love. But the best way to decide whether you think the Bible is important, whether you think that it is the Word of God, whether you think that it is true, is to start reading it.

We need to move from asking "How should I read the Bible?" as though there is one right way to read it and one right message or answer to find, and ask instead, "How can I read the Bible?" What are the many tools and methods and practices that will enable and empower us to read the Bible for ourselves?

Get the right tools

To read the Bible you need a Bible that you can read. This sounds simple, but many people have Bibles in their homes that they find confusing or boring. You won't read the Bible if it isn't approachable to you. So find a Bible that you love. Try a bunch of different Bibles before you settle. A Bible is very much a personal preference! Here are some suggestions:

❖ **A New Revised Standard Version (NRSV) Study Bible.** These Bibles have notes with further explanations about the culture and background of the text that many people find interesting and helpful.

New Interpreter's Study Bible and *Oxford Annotated Study Bible* are two good ones.

❖ ***The Message*** by Eugene Peterson. This is a modern rendering that is much easier to read than many traditional translations. It's a good place to start if you find the language of the Bible intimidating.

❖ **The New Jerusalem Bible**. If you like poetry, this is a very poetic, beautiful translation that is also very accurate.

❖ **Any Bible you like**. If the "thees" and "thous" of King James do it for you—read that!

Many people also find other tools helpful for Bible reading. These include:

❖ **A Bible reading schedule.** Some Bibles are broken up into chunks for daily reading, so that you'll read the whole thing in a year. There are also schedules you can use with your existing Bible to read the whole book in a year. Check out *The Bible Challenge* by Marek Zabriski for a year-long plan to read the entire Bible.

❖ ***Forward Day by Day*** (available in print, by email, or online, as a podcast, a smartphone app, or on a website) has daily Bible readings and a meditation.

❖ **Bible study resources.** If you want to read a particular book of the Bible, there's probably a companion book available that can provide helpful explanations and further information.

❖ **Electronic resources:** Many groups will send you a verse a day by email or send you big portions of scripture each day so that you can read the entire Bible in a year using your email. If you are a computer person, this may be a way to make Bible reading more doable for you.

Set a goal. Just like all other practices of life, you have to make reading the Bible a priority and make time for it. A few years ago, my spouse decided to run a marathon. She didn't just run 26.2 miles the very next day. She had to come up with a training plan and work on her running a bit each day for several months. Reading the Bible is not as hard as running a marathon, but it still requires a plan and a commitment.

Pick a time of day you'd like to do this. Many find it easy to link reading the Bible to prayer time, either before or after. Then set a goal for what you'd like to read. Do you just want to focus on one verse each day? Would you like to set a goal of reading one "book" of the Bible a month? Do you desire to try to read the entire Bible in a year?

And lest you think that you don't have time to read the Bible, consider this: The average American household watches television around forty hours a week. You can read the Old and New Testaments out loud in just seventy-four hours. If you read the Bible instead of watching television for two weeks, you could read the entire Bible cover to cover!

When you start reading the Bible, you'll need to pick an approach. Reading the Bible for any reason is great, but you probably want to "get something out of it." Plowing through the reading just to do it is not going to seem fulfilling. Instead, pick your approach to the biblical text.

❖ **Do you want to see what the Bible says to you, today?** Then after you read each day, spend some time reflecting on some questions. How does what I read touch my life today? What might God be saying to me here? Have I ever felt like this/had an experience like this/ known of a situation like this? What does this Bible reading teach me about that feeling/experience/situation?

❖ **Do you want to learn more about what the Bible meant in its own time?** Choose an annotated study Bible. Read the passage. Then read all the notes/footnotes that your Bible has on that passage. Read the passage again.

❖ **Do you want the Bible to be an intimate part of your life?** Pick a verse or passage and read it multiple times a day for a week. Intentionally try to memorize it. Or read scripture repetitively. With your daily reading, try this method:

- Read the passage through once aloud.

- Reflect on what word or phrase jumped out at you. Write it down.

- Read the passage through again aloud.

- Ask yourself, "Where does this passage touch my life, today?"

- Read the passage through again aloud.

- Ask yourself, "How am I being called to change in response to what I've heard?"

Start somewhere. Once you have your goal and your approach, you have to decide where to start. Here are some recommendations:

❖ If you just want to do some Bible reading but don't necessarily want to read the entire Bible in a set amount of time, start with the Gospel of Luke. Read one chapter every day. After you've finished Luke, try Acts or Genesis. Then move on from there.

❖ Don't start at the beginning and think you'll read the whole way through. Ninety percent of people (who aren't weird like me) will stop reading in Leviticus.

❖ If you want to read the entire Bible in a year (or two years—there are plans for that as well), pick your plan (online, printed schedule, daily reading Bible). Then pick a start date (you don't have to start on January 1!).

Before you start reading the Bible, cultivate the right attitude for the journey. The most important thing about reading the Bible is not how smart you are or how many resources you have but the openness with which you approach the Bible and your willingness to be challenged and changed by it. You'll know you're reading the Bible properly when you are not always comfortable (if you're always on the "right" side, then you're not reading it deeply).

> The reason the Bible has spoken to so many people in so many ways over all these years is because it is rich and dense with meaning.

You are reading the Bible well when you don't always understand it, or when you come back to the same passage and it seems to have changed while you were away. The reason the Bible has spoken to so many people in so many ways over all these years is because it is rich and dense with meaning. If you're able to "get it" in one sitting, then you probably aren't reading it deeply. You know you're reading well when you are humbled by the text, and you want to read more.

The Bible has words to say to us, inspiration for our lives, lessons to learn, encouragement to receive, wisdom to enlighten. It offers a window of revelation into how God has related to humanity in the past, and it offers us a window into the heart of God's internal life as well.

The Bible is not just a book

The Bible is the breath of God. "All scripture is inspired by God and is useful for teaching, for reproof, for correction, and for training in righteousness, so that everyone who belongs to God may be proficient, equipped for every good work" (2 Timothy 3:16-17). The word "inspired" is literally "God-breathed."

The Bible is a living thing. "Indeed, the word of God is living and active, sharper than any two-edged sword, piercing until it divides soul from spirit, joints from marrow; it is able to judge the thoughts and intentions of the heart" (Hebrews 4:12).

There is a tradition in Judaism and Christianity that you treat scripture (Bibles or Torah scrolls) the same way you would treat a human body—when it is worn out, you either bury it or burn it. This reverence teaches us something about the way in which we should view this book, not because the pages themselves are sacred, but because the Word they convey is sacred.

So give the Bible a chance. Let it breathe on you. Let it come alive for you.

Blessed Lord, who caused all holy Scriptures to be written for our learning: Grant us so to hear them, read, mark, learn, and inwardly digest them, that we may embrace and ever hold fast the blessed hope of everlasting life, which you have given us in our Savior Jesus Christ; who lives and reigns with you and the Holy Spirit, one God, for ever and ever. Amen.

(*The Book of Common Prayer*, p. 236)

Reflection questions

❖ Have you ever or recently read the Bible? How did it go?

❖ Have you ever read anything in the Bible that has changed the way you act or behave?

❖ Have you ever experienced something that was "true" even if it wasn't factual?

❖ How does it change your understanding of the Bible to think of it as "God-breathed" or as a living thing?

DOES GOD
ANSWER PRAYER?

Almighty God, the fountain of all wisdom, you know our necessities before we ask and our ignorance in asking: Have compassion on our weakness, and mercifully give us those things which for our unworthiness we dare not, and for our blindness we cannot ask; through the worthiness of your Son Jesus Christ our Lord, who lives and reigns with you and the Holy Spirit, one God, now and for ever. Amen.

(*The Book of Common Prayer*, p. 231)

Not long ago, I was waiting for the elevator one morning in the building where I live. One of my neighbors, who I don't

know by name, stepped out of her apartment at about the same moment. We were both, perhaps, on our way to work. Eyeing my clerical collar, she asked, "Are you a priest?" Yes, I answered. "Well," she said. "I have a quick question. Why doesn't God answer all prayers? Does prayer really work?"

Talk about an elevator speech! I had just a few seconds to answer one of the hardest questions any person of faith must reckon with. This is such a tough, tough question, because a person asking that question is often a person in pain, someone who is struggling with something difficult, someone who is suffering. And we must always, always tread carefully in tending the hearts and souls of those who are suffering and in pain. But the question is also tough because it centers on a misconception about what prayer is and what prayer is for.

Most of us, most of the time, see prayer as one of a few things:

❖ It's something we do on Sundays—that thing we do when we go to church. Prayer is not something that's embedded in our daily lives.

❖ It's something we do by rote, like checking something off a list. I grew up praying a series of rote prayers— "Now I lay me down to sleep" at bedtime, a family grace at mealtime, the same words every Sunday at church. Those prayers often become akin to saying the Pledge of Allegiance...it's just something you do.

❖ There's a funny (and completely irreverent) Youtube series called Mr. Deity. In one of the episodes, God is sitting on a couch reading a book. He picks up his cell phone and calls his voicemail, which informs him he has 2,999,672,581 voicemails. He starts listening to a few of them (a table grace, someone in the hospital, someone using the Lord's name in vain) and then just deletes all the messages. It's funny, but it exposes a truth about how we view prayer. We often think of praying as leaving a voicemail—no one's listening, but maybe if we leave a message, God will get back to us.

❖ Perhaps the biggest misconception about prayer is that we see God as a holy vending machine. We say our prayers, which is like putting our money in the machine. We press the buttons, and we want our candy bar to come out. Then we're angry and disappointed when it doesn't, or we decide that God doesn't really answer prayers.

None of these things is how the Bible — or especially how Jesus — describes and sees prayer. Throughout the Bible,

PRAYERS IN THE BIBLE

- When the land finally dries after the flood, the first thing Noah does is offer sacrificial prayers to God (Genesis 8:20-21).

- As soon as Moses and the Israelites safely cross through the Red Sea, they pray to God in song (Exodus 15).

- Central to our Bible is the book of Psalms, a record of prayers written when people felt all kinds of emotions—joy, sadness, anger, fear, disappointment, relief.

  ◇ Answer me when I call, O God of my right!
    You gave me room when I was in distress.
    Be gracious to me, and hear my prayer.
    (Psalm 4:1)

  ◇ O Lord, in the morning you hear my voice
    in the morning I plead my case to you, and
    watch. (Psalm 5:3)

  ◇ Hear a just cause, O Lord; attend to my cry;
    give ear to my prayer from lips free of deceit.
    (Psalm 17:1)

- When people encounter angels or Jesus in the New Testament, they often respond with spontaneous prayer (frequently in the form of songs).

◇ Mary's Song of Praise, the *Magnificat* (Luke 1:46-56)

◇ Zechariah's Song, the *Benedictus* (Luke 1: 67-79)

◇ Simeon's Song, the *Nunc Dimmitis* (Luke 2:25-32)

• Paul, in his letters, tells us that he prays at all times and in all circumstances and urges all believers to do the same. (1 Thessalonians 5:16-18, Philippians 4:6-7)

prayer is central. It is foundational. Indeed, prayer is the most important activity in our lives. Wherever we look in the Bible, we read examples of people who see prayer not as an isolated action, a rote response, a voicemail, or a vending machine, but as a way of life.

Prayer is first mentioned in Genesis, as early in creation, "people began to invoke the name of the Lord" (4:26). Scripture offers countless examples of prayer—people in various circumstances, places, and times described as praying. Sometimes we even get to read the words of their prayers. Prayers are scattered throughout the Old and New Testaments: from the song of Miriam in Exodus to the Song of Mary (the *Magnificat*) in Luke. Most of the psalms are sung prayers.

In the letter of James, we find powerful encouragement for believers to offer prayers, in good times and in bad. James' invitation to prayer is lovely: "Are any among you suffering? They should pray. Are any cheerful? They should sing songs of praise. Are any among you sick? They should call for the elders of the church and have them pray over them, anointing them with oil in the name of the Lord. The prayer of faith will save the sick, and the Lord will raise them up; and anyone who has committed sins will be forgiven. Therefore confess your sins to one another, and pray for one another, so that you may be healed. The prayer of the righteous is powerful and effective" (James 5:13-16).

Most importantly for Christians, Jesus prays. Prayer is so important to Jesus that he, personally, regularly took time away to do it. Let's look at just three examples:

❖ In the morning, while it was still very dark, he got up and went out to a deserted place, and there he prayed. (Mark 1:35)

❖ Now during those days he went out to the mountain to pray; and he spent the night in prayer to God. (Luke 6:12)

❖ Then he withdrew from them about a stone's throw, knelt down, and prayed, "Father, if you are willing, remove this cup from me; yet, not my will but yours be done." Then an angel from heaven appeared to him and gave him strength. In his anguish he prayed more earnestly, and his sweat became like great drops of blood falling down on the ground. (Luke 22:41-44)

Prayer wasn't just something Jesus recommended for others or only for the disciples, but something he did often. Jesus was continually taking time from his busy schedule of teaching, preaching, and healing to PRAY, of all things. And Jesus assumes that we will all take prayer as seriously as he does. In Matthew 6:7-13, when Jesus teaches his disciples to pray, he says "when you pray," not "if you pray."

Jesus, by his life and teaching, tells us that prayer is not a once-a-week obligation, something we check off a list, a voicemail that we leave, or a payment

> Prayer is a conversation. Prayer is part of a relationship.

in a holy vending machine, but a conversation that takes place in relationship. So what do we mean by that? Well, prayer is a conversation, and prayer is part of a relationship.

Let's say that again. Prayer is a conversation. Prayer is part of a relationship.

One of the best parts of my day is the end of it, when I can sit down with my spouse, talk to him about my day and listen to him talk about his. Maybe you do this too—talking at the end of the day or the end of the week to a spouse, sibling, parent, or beloved friend. It's a simple thing, but it's the time when we share our lives with one another—the good, the bad, and the ugly. Sometimes we ask for advice or input. Sometimes we convey information. Sometimes we share feelings and seek support. Sometimes we simply tell stories about things that happened. Our conversation is usually punctuated by times of comfortable silence, as we sit together and enjoy one another's presence.

That is what prayer is like—a conversation in relationship.

- ❖ Prayer involves both talking and listening, as you share your life.

- ❖ Prayer involves times of comfortable silence.

- ❖ Prayer is not always about getting answers to questions or about receiving things.

In fact, it would be pretty damaging if I approached my relationship with my spouse like a vending machine. What if

- ❖ Every time I talked to him, I was asking for something?

- ❖ I ignored him in the time in between, when I didn't need something?

❖ I was always upset when he didn't give me exactly what I wanted?

I'm fairly certain our relationship would be deeply damaged if either one of us approached it that way.

The same is true with God. We need to approach our prayer, our conversation with God, in the way that we approach a relationship with a loved one—not the way that we approach an obligation or a machine.

And that's why the question "Does God answer prayer?" is the wrong question—or at least not the best question. This question assumes that prayer is a one-way street. It assumes that prayer is about bringing questions to be answered. This question assumes that prayer is about bringing problems to be solved or, worse, bringing demands to be met.

Modern mystical writer Kathleen Norris says, "Prayer is not asking for what we think we want, but asking to be changed in ways we cannot imagine." Said another way, Phillip Yancey writes, "The real value of persistent prayer is not so much that we get what we want as that we become the person we should be."

When we change our perspective, we begin to ask not, "Does God answer prayer?" but "Does God meet me in prayer?" The answer to that question is a resounding "Yes!"

God promises to show up, to meet us in prayer, to be present in relationship.

> For God to meet us in prayer, we must also meet God in prayer.

Of course, no relationship can be one-sided. Imagine being in a dating relationship. But every time you schedule a date with that person, he stands you up. The person has a long list of excuses: he got caught up at work, her parent was sick, he got a flat tire. Each time, you give her the benefit of the doubt, and go again to meet for the date. But each time, he doesn't show up.

That's a pretty one-sided relationship that doesn't have much of a future. And that's what it's like when we don't approach our prayer to God as a part of our relationship with God. For God to meet us in prayer, we must also meet God in prayer. We have to show up. We must make prayer a priority in our lives, even in the midst of busy schedules and competing demands. We have to make space for our relationship with God.

So how can we do that? How can we begin or enrich our life of prayer? How can we make space for God in our lives, in our homes, in our calendars, and in our hearts?

Let us share a few tips and tricks for a life of prayer. There's no right way for everyone to pray, so you might have to try for a while to find the right ways for you to pray.

❖ **Set a time (when)**. Yes, just like everything else, you have to make time for prayer. It's not going to happen if you aren't intentional. Any relationship will wither and die if you don't purposefully set aside time to be together—and relationship with God is no different. Set a goal for time set aside to pray (5, 10, 15, 30 minutes). Start small. After some practice, increase your time. Pick a time of day that works for you—first thing in the morning before everyone is up, last thing at night, while you're in the car, or when you're on your lunch break. Know yourself and your schedule. Don't always give God your "leftovers" (the time when you are drained and worn out; the time left over when you've already given time to everyone and everything else).

❖ **Find a place (where)**. It's hard to pray if you're being constantly interrupted, or if the place you are praying isn't conducive to prayer. Having a special chair or a place set aside in your home can really help. Try setting a mood (lighting a candle) or even going outside. Whatever you do, choose a place that works for you.

❖ **Keep a list (who and what)**. Some prayers will come unprompted, as things you didn't even know you were thinking about rise to the surface, but you also might need your memory jogged. Keep a list of people and things you have been asked to pray for (you could even start with a church bulletin). When something arises during your day that is troublesome or delightful, jot yourself a note. It's a good reminder to share that thing with God during your prayer time. Allow time for unprompted prayer as well. Don't stop praying as soon as you've gotten through your list.

Just as important—perhaps even more important—than when, where, who, and what, you have to decide how you'll pray. There are as many forms of prayer as there are people on earth, and your prayer doesn't even have to include any words. "Prayer is responding to God, by thought and by deeds, with or without words" (*The Book of Common Prayer*, p. 856).

❖ **Spoken prayer can take many forms.** These include adoration, praise, thanksgiving, penitence, oblation, intercession, and petition (See *The Book of Common Prayer*, pp. 856-857). Our prayers need not (and should not) be only a list of requests for ourselves or on behalf of others. We can spend time enjoying God's presence, praising God's being, thanking God for blessings, confessing to God our failures, offering ourselves fully to God, and bringing our needs and the needs of others into God's presence. In fact, many people find the ACTS form of prayer helpful (adoration, confession, thanksgiving, supplication), finding that going in that order helps prayer to be rightly oriented and not focused on our needs or wants alone.

❖ **Scripted and extemporaneous prayer.** In The Episcopal Church, we often use formal, written prayers. The words of these prayers are beautiful and ancient and can help make space for an awareness of God's presence. But it's also okay to use extemporaneous prayers—using our own words, as though having a conversation with God. Try to integrate both into your prayer life.

❖ **Remember, you can also pray without words!** There are dozens of active or creative forms of prayer—journaling, music, walking a labyrinth, art, praying "in color," and doing chores as a way of praying are some examples.

❖ **Start with your comfort zone.** Are you a talker? Talk to God out loud on a walk (ignore what other people think!). Are you a writer? Try journaling. Love music? Try singing or listening to music as part of your prayer life. If you start with your own passions, you are likely to find your way into a life-giving form of prayer, as the thing that you love doing connects you to the God of Love.

❖ **Challenge yourself to pray in new ways.**
Although you might start in your comfort zone, don't always pray "the way you've always done it." Your prayer life will get stale, and you'll likely fall into routine at the expense of relationship. Set a goal to occasionally add a new or different practice to your prayer life so that you can meet God in new and different ways.

If you're not sure where to start a new life of constant prayer, here are some easy ways to pray.

❖ **Start with grace at meals.** Commit to pray at every meal, every time (even when you are eating out!). If you're not sure what words to say, there are prayers in *The Book of Common Prayer* (p. 835). If you offer up prayers every time you eat, you'll already be praying at least three times a day!

❖ **Start a practice with your family.** Decide together to pray at bedtime or to use meal times to talk about the day. This is actually an ancient kind of prayer called *examen*. Go deeper than just "What happened?" Ask things like: "Where did you meet God today?" or "Where did you fall short today?" or "When did you feel the Holy Spirit today?" If you engage in this practice as a family, you are more likely to support one another.

❖ **Try to do something that you do daily with greater intention, as a way of prayer.** From the earliest centuries of Christianity, monks and nuns have said that anything can be a prayer as long as you direct your action toward God. Driving your car? Turn off the radio and pray for each person you see (especially the ones who cut you off!) as well as those on your prayer list. Doing dishes? Thank God for all the blessings that make that possible (the food you ate, the hands that grew and prepared it, the warm water). Wash the dishes as though you are washing Jesus' feet. Literally anything you do can be prayer, as long as you are doing that thing with God.

Whatever you do, be generous with yourself. Pray as you are, not as you aren't. Don't force yourself to follow someone

> Prayer is a practice, something you learn by doing.

else's example of prayer, if it isn't working for you. You are created to have a relationship with God, a unique relationship that won't follow the exact pattern of anyone else's relationship with God. Pray as you can, not as you can't. You don't have to get everything in your life right in order to start praying. Don't wait until you're sure, or you've memorized the right words, or you have your life under control. Just start, and the rest will follow. God is there, wishing and waiting for you to show up.

The important thing about prayer is to keep at it. Prayer is a practice, something you learn by doing. So right now, we invite you to give it a shot, and start, or continue, your conversation and your relationship with God.

Almighty, everlasting God, let our prayer in your sight be as incense, the lifting up of our hands as the evening sacrifice. Give us grace to behold you, present in your Word and Sacraments, and to recognize you in the lives of those around us. Stir up in us the flame of that love which burned in the heart of your Son as he bore his passion, and let it burn in us to eternal life and to the ages of ages. Amen.

(*The Book of Common Prayer*, p. 113)

Reflection questions

❖ What was your childhood experience of prayer? Is that the same or different as your experience of prayer today?

❖ What about prayer is difficult for you?

❖ Does thinking about prayer as a conversation in relationship, rather than questions to be answered, change your understanding of prayer? How so or why not?

❖ Prayer happens in many different forms. Is there a different way of praying that you would like to try? What goals could you set to make that possible?

WHY DO BAD THINGS HAPPEN?

O merciful Father, who has taught us in your holy Word that you do not willingly afflict or grieve the children of men: Look with pity upon the sorrows of your servants for whom our prayers are offered. Remember them, O Lord, in mercy, nourish their souls with patience, comfort them with a sense of your goodness, lift up your countenance upon them, and give them peace; through Jesus Christ our Lord. Amen.

(*The Book of Common Prayer*, p. 831)

Quite often, our most meaningful conversations about religion address the question "why?" Why does evil exist? Why is there so much suffering and pain? Why do bad things happen to good people?

These are questions that all of us have asked at one time or another—after an inexplicable accident or a devastating diagnosis, an untimely death or a natural disaster. In these kinds of circumstances, it is understandable, natural, and human to ask "why?!" And that "why?" is a fundamental question of faith. We are forced to ask "why?" because what we see in the world comes into conflict with what we believe about God.

Traditionally, people have believed that God is:

❖ omnipotent: all-powerful

❖ omniscient: all-knowing

❖ omnibenevolent: all-loving; all-good

But if God is all-powerful, all-knowing, and all-good, then why do bad things happen to good people? Wouldn't an all-loving, all-good God want to remove all suffering and pain? And if God wants to remove all suffering and pain, wouldn't an all-powerful God be able to do so?

We are not, of course, the first people to ask these kinds of questions. This has always been a fundamental question of faith. In fact, there is even a name for this kind of questioning: theodicy. Theodicy is the branch of theology and philosophy that attempts to reconcile the existence of evil and suffering with what we know and believe about God. Theodicy is church-speak for asking the question "why?"

Over the centuries, Christians have come up with lots of answers to that question, some far less satisfactory than others. Let's look at some of them.

1. People deserve what they get and get what they deserve—God causes people to suffer because of something they did, because of some sin they committed.

Biblical support

> Tell the innocent how fortunate they are, for they shall eat the fruit of their labors. Woe to the guilty! How unfortunate they are, for what their hands have done shall be done to them. (Isaiah 3:10-11)

> No harm happens to the righteous, but the wicked are filled with trouble. (Proverbs 12:21)

Example

We've all heard instances of this, right? Sometimes we hear people say they believe that something bad has happened because of something they did wrong. We might have the belief that an illness is punishment for not having gone to church enough or served the poor enough. This causes nagging doubt when something bad happens: "What did I do wrong?"

Benefits

The world is orderly and comprehensible—there is a logical relationship between what we do and what happens to us. We can then maintain an image of God as all-loving, all-powerful, and totally in control. It justifies God. In fact, a lot of us secretly like this explanation, because it helps us believe that "bad" people will get what they deserve!

Problems

This isn't terribly comforting to a grieving person. It teaches people to blame themselves and creates guilt. This theory goes against our experience: we see people who do bad and aren't punished and people who are seemingly good and suffer greatly.

2. People may not get what they deserve in this world, but they will "get it in the end!" The scales of justice are balanced in the afterlife. This is a variation of the "people get what they deserve," but it extends the timeline.

Biblical support

The Rich Man and Lazarus
Luke 16:19-31

There was a rich man who was dressed in purple and fine linen and who feasted sumptuously every day. And at his gate lay a poor man named Lazarus, covered with sores, who longed to satisfy his hunger with what fell from the rich man's table; even the dogs would come and lick his sores. The poor man died and was carried away by the angels to be with Abraham. The rich man also died and was buried. In Hades, where he was being tormented, he looked up and saw Abraham far away with Lazarus by his side. He called out, "Father Abraham, have mercy on me, and send Lazarus to dip the tip of his finger in water and cool my tongue; for I am in agony in these flames." But Abraham said, "Child, remember that during your lifetime you received your good things, and Lazarus in like manner evil things; but now he is comforted here, and you are in agony. Besides all this, between you and us a great chasm has been fixed, so that those who might want to pass from here to you cannot do so, and no one can cross from there to us." He said, "Then, father, I beg you to send him to my father's house—for I have five brothers—that he may warn them, so that they will not also come into this place of torment." Abraham replied, "They have Moses and the prophets; they should listen to them." He said, "No, father Abraham; but if someone goes to them from the dead, they will repent." He said to him, "If they do not listen to Moses and the prophets, neither will they be convinced even if someone rises from the dead."

Example

Those who continue to do bad and yet prosper in this world will get their punishment when they meet God. Good people who suffer will eventually receive their reward, even if we don't see it in this earthly life.

Benefits

All the same benefits as the first explanation, just a longer timeline.

Problems

When we push punishment into the realm of eternity, God's goodness comes back into question. Is eternal punishment really a "just" response to wrongs done in this world?

3. Evil and sin are really merely a privation of good; evil is not a thing in itself. Evil and sin are actually just a lack of the good. God is all-good, and evil is the absence of good. Human beings

and all things were created good, but any choice away from God or the good is evil. This view is championed by Augustine of Hippo and, to a certain extent, by Thomas Aquinas.

Biblical support

> God saw everything that he had made, and indeed, it was very good. And there was evening and there was morning, the sixth day. (Genesis 1:31)

> No one, when tempted, should say, "I am being tempted by God"; for God cannot be tempted by evil and he himself tempts no one. (James 1:13)

Example

Hungry children around the world exist because of the absence of enough good. That is what we call "evil." If there were enough good, as people responded with love and concern to share what they have with others, then there would be no more hunger.

Benefits

This reconciles our beliefs about a supremely good God with the existence of evil. Evil is simply a gap between what is and what ought to be. Most of us know and understand that things are not "as they ought to be" in the world, and evil is our experience of that reality.

Problems

Does "absence of good" really explain the horrors of the Holocaust? Evil in many parts of scripture is portrayed as an active force rather than as an absence. And finally, there is a practical concern: could you really say this to someone suffering?

4. God has a reason for suffering; it teaches us, or other people, something. In fact, some would go so far as to say that suffering is part of what purifies us and forms us into the people that we are called to be. This view is championed by Irenaeus.

Biblical support

> For the LORD reproves the one he loves, as a father the son in whom he delights. (Proverbs 3:12)

> See, I have refined you, but not like silver; I have tested you in the furnace of adversity. (Isaiah 48:10)

Example

Think of a person who suffers from a degenerative disease, but believes that it makes her (or someone around her) into a better person. Think of the person who, after the loss of a limb, turns around his life and does amazing things for others.

Benefits

It gives suffering higher purpose. It sanctifies suffering and makes it holy. It makes the times when we suffer bearable, because it means that some good might come from our pain. We experience this as true. Sometimes personal suffering gives us a deeper capacity for compassion.

Problems

This condones individual pain as part of a higher purpose; it justifies those who cause suffering and evil. If a human purposely inflicts pain on someone in order to "make them better" or "teach them," we would put them in jail. Why do we think it would be okay for God to do that? This also may not be a good answer for someone suffering. Rather than allowing them to acknowledge the real pain and horror of their suffering, this view makes them feel like they have to see their suffering as "good."

5. Human free choice causes suffering in the world. This is called the free will defense, and it's advocated by American philosopher Alvin Plantinga. It proposes that human freedom is the greatest good. God's gift of freedom means that sometimes people will choose erroneously, misusing that freedom to commit evil acts. Still, it is better to have freedom than a world of robots that would be "forced" to choose good all the time.

Biblical support

Surely, this commandment that I am commanding you today is not too hard for you, nor is it too far away. It is not in heaven, that you should say, "Who will go up to heaven for us, and get it for us so that we may hear it and observe it?" Neither is it beyond the sea, that you should say, "Who will cross to the other side of the sea for us, and get it for us so that we may hear it and observe it?" No, the word is very near to you; it is in your mouth and in your heart for you to observe. See, I have set before you today life and prosperity, death and adversity. If you obey the commandments of the LORD your God that I am commanding you today, by loving the LORD your God, walking in his ways, and observing his commandments, decrees, and ordinances, then you shall live and become numerous, and the LORD your God will bless you in the land that you are entering to possess. But if your heart turns away and you do not hear, but are led astray to bow down to other gods and serve them, I declare to you today that you shall perish; you shall not live long in the land that you are crossing the Jordan to enter and possess. I call heaven and earth to witness against you today that I have set before you life and death, blessings and curses. Choose life so that you and your descendants may live. (Deuteronomy 30:11-19)

Example

It all goes back to the garden, where Adam and Eve were given free will and allowed the choice—to eat or not.

Benefits

This view explains the evil that we see—and the reality that people often choose against the good, causing bad things to happen to themselves and others. We don't have to blame God for the bad things that happen.

Problems

Does human choice explain all the evil in the world? What about diseases or natural disasters? Couldn't an all-powerful God have somehow created people who had freedom of choice but who would always choose good?

6. What we mistakenly see as "evil" is just beyond our limited, human understanding. The larger and wider tapestry of God's plan in the world is beyond our scope of understanding. So what we see as evil is just our myopic view of the wider working of God. Think about seeing a tapestry from the front versus from the back or not backing up enough to see the beautiful art.

Biblical support

> But Joseph said to them, "Do not be afraid! Am I in the place of God? Even though you intended to do harm to me, God intended it for good, in order to preserve a numerous people, as he is doing today." (Genesis 50:19-20)

Examples

Imagine a man screaming in pain as others huddle over him. It seems cruel at first. But if we step back, we see that the people huddling over the person are medical professionals setting a broken bone, and the scene takes place in an emergency room. What initially seemed heartless turns out to be a healing gesture. The evil doesn't disappear; it is still there (just ask the man!), but the problem of evil is no longer present because the intention is good. The ancient theologian Origen understood the betrayal of Judas in this way. Judas' betrayal of Jesus was a necessary part in the "tapestry" of God's salvation.

Benefits

It allows for our suffering to be redeemed, if it's ultimately working toward a greater good. It underscores the connectedness of humanity and time and place, taking the "long view."

Problems

It is offensive to someone suffering to say, "This looks like good if you see it from the other side!" Are we really willing to say that great evils like genocide are "good" when seen from another angle?

7. God does not cause our suffering. It happens for some reason other than the will of God.

Biblical support

The book of Job is a long poem that essentially explores the nature of evil and suffering. The book begins with a conversation in the heavens, when Satan tells God that the only reason that Job is faithful is because his life is going well. Satan then uses his powers to test Job. The suffering that comes to Job as he loses his wealth and his children and even his own health is not caused by God; it is caused by Satan, the adversary.

Example

People make this argument when they claim that the evil they have done is because Satan, the devil, tempted them to do it: "The devil made me do it."

Benefits

We don't have to blame God or ourselves for the suffering in the world. We can stop asking "why" and start figuring out what to do in this new situation.

Problems

Does this mean that God is not omnipotent? How do we understand the power of God? Can God do anything? Is God capable of doing the impossible? That is, is anything impossible for God? Are there such things as mutually exclusive possibilities with God (i.e. that God create a rock so heavy that God cannot move it?) C.S. Lewis says, "It is no more possible for God than for the weakest of his creatures to carry out both of two mutually exclusive alternatives; not because God's power meets an obstacle, but because nonsense remains nonsense even when we talk it about God" (*Problem of Pain*). If God doesn't cause suffering, does God allow it? And is that, in the end, any different?

We have a lot of possible answers to the question of "why?" Some are more satisfying than others. Each of these has its benefits and problems. It is perhaps unsatisfying, but true, that the question of "why" does not have an easy or obvious answer. It is one of those questions that we will wrestle with in this life, and, in the age to come, we hope we can ask God face-to-face.

Rabbi Irving Greenburg writes that "why" is not the only, or perhaps the best, question to ask in the face of unspeakable suffering.

> It's hard to speak of a loving God, it's hard to speak of even being in the image of God, infinitely valuable and unique, in a world in which babies

WHY DO BAD THINGS HAPPEN?

were burned alive by the Nazis and no one lifted a finger, in which people were gassed en masse. For example, there was a department of the SS that was in charge of bringing down the price of that gassing to make human life even cheaper. How do you speak, then, of a God who treasures humans or, in Christian terms, of a God who loved the world so much he would sacrifice his own son, and yet, here it is that, to save a half a penny's worth of gas, people were burned alive? The answer is, it's very hard, and for many Jews, it has been a crisis of faith. In the presence of burning children, how could one talk of a loving God? I once wrote that no theological statement should be made that would not be credible in the presence of burning children. What could you say about God when a child is burning alive? My answer is there's nothing to say. If there's anything you can do, jump into that pit and pull the child out. And if you can heal that child, if you can pour oil on their burns, then you are making a statement about God... But you have to live in the contradiction... I would constantly torment myself, "Where was God? Where was God?" Then one day it hit me very powerfully that, if I was suffering this way and I hadn't been in the Holocaust, how much more in a certain sense was God suffering? If a human felt this pain, what did an infinite consciousness feel?

I think that was a turning point in my personal religious development, because I suddenly felt a certain sense, if I can say so, of compassion or maybe even pity for God, and an overwhelming sense, suddenly, that this God had not stopped the Holocaust maybe because this God was suffering and wanted me to stop the Holocaust. As a Jew, I always hesitate to use language of God suffering, because it seems to be a Christian patent. But it's not so. I came to see this has been a central belief of the Jewish people—that God shares our pain. Indeed, Christianity was never more Jewish than when it expressed it in those terms—that God suffers with humans. I said to myself I'd asked the wrong question when I asked where was God? The answer was obvious: where else would God be, but suffering with God's people?"[1]

Rabbi Greenburg reminds us of an incredibly important point—asking "why" is important. But trying to answer the question of "why?"—especially in the face of one who is suffering—is at best, hubristic, and, at worst, incredibly damaging. It is our right, perhaps our need, to ask the question "why?" when we, ourselves, are suffering.

---

1 "Easing the Divine Suffering" by Rabbi Irving Greenberg in *The Life of Meaning: Reflections on Faith, Doubt, and Repairing the World* edited by Bob Abernathy. Permission requested.

But we must be very careful about proposing our own answers in the face of other people's suffering. For both ourselves and for others, we might need to learn to ask some different questions.

> Where else would God be, but suffering with God's people?

We need to move from "why?" to "where?" Where is God when suffering happens?

Let's look at some biblical verses about where God is when there is earthly suffering.

Then Nebuchadnezzar was so filled with rage against Shadrach, Meshach, and Abednego that his face was distorted. He ordered the furnace to be heated up seven times more than was customary, and ordered some of the strongest guards in his army to bind Shadrach, Meshach, and Abednego and to throw them into the furnace of blazing fire. So the men were bound, still wearing their tunics, their trousers, their hats, and their other garments, and they were thrown into the furnace of blazing fire. Because the king's command was urgent and the furnace was so overheated, the raging flames killed the men who lifted Shadrach, Meshach, and Abednego. But the three men, Shadrach, Meshach, and Abednego, fell down, bound, into the furnace of blazing fire. Then King Nebuchadnezzar was astonished and rose up quickly. He said to his counsellors, "Was it not three men that we threw bound into the fire?" They answered the king, "True, O king." He replied, "But I see four men unbound, walking in the middle of the fire, and they are not hurt; and the fourth has the appearance of a god." (Daniel 3:19-25)

Even though I walk through the darkest valley, I fear no evil; for you are with me; your rod and your staff—they comfort me. (Psalm 23:4)

For I am convinced that neither death, nor life, nor angels, nor rulers, nor things present, nor things to come, nor powers, nor height, nor depth, nor anything else in all creation, will be able to separate us from the love of God in Christ Jesus our Lord. (Romans 8:38-39)

To the question "Where is God?", Christians proclaim Emmanuel, "God is with us." When we say that, we aren't just talking about a baby being born in a manger. We are talking about God, our God, being born as a vulnerable, naked, helpless human baby—coming into this scary, broken, tragic world that we live in.

As Christians we proclaim that our God became human, lived, suffered, and died an untimely death so that we would never again have to go through the brokenness and grief and suffering and death of this world alone.

Where is God when bad things happen? God is with each person who dies, for God has died before. God is with each family who grieves, for God knows the grief and loss of a child. God is with each of us who mourns and questions and yearns and longs for a world where this is not possible, for God mourns and questions and yearns and longs for that world as well.

It is understandable, normal, excusable, perhaps even required that humans ask the question of "why?" We join the ranks of centuries of faithful people when we do so, when we wrestle with God and engage deeply this fundamental question of our faith. But it is inexcusable if we let our questions stop there. If we ask "why?" we must also be prepared to ask "where?" Where is God in the midst of suffering and pain?

And then, perhaps we can ask the further questions, those that demand something, not of God, but of us: "what?" and "how?" What am I being called to do in response to the evil of this world? How can I respond to the suffering that I encounter?

Gracious God, the comfort of all who sorrow, the strength of all who suffer: Let the cry of those in misery and need come to you, that they may find your mercy present with them in all their afflictions; and give us, we pray, the strength to serve them for the sake of him who suffered for us, your Son Jesus Christ our Lord. Amen.

(*The Book of Common Prayer*, p. 279)

Reflection questions

❖ Which of the answers to "Why does evil and suffering exist?" do you find most compelling? How does that answer work for you?

❖ At a time when you were struggling, have you had someone give you an "answer" that was unsatisfying or hurtful? What was that experience like?

❖ All of the different "answers" for the presence of suffering and evil are supported by Bible verses. What might the presence of so many different answers in the scriptures say to us? Does it surprise you to see so many different ways of understanding suffering and evil in the Bible?

❖ How might what you've read inform the way that you interact with people who are suffering? What are some ways that we can be with people who are in pain without diminishing or explaining away their experience?

❖ Have you ever had an experience of God's presence with you in a time of suffering or pain (your own or someone else's)? How did that experience inform your understanding of suffering?

WHERE DO I GO WHEN I DIE?

Almighty God, who through your only-begotten Son Jesus Christ overcame death and opened to us the gate of everlasting life: Grant that we, who celebrate with joy the day of the Lord's resurrection, may be raised from the death of sin by your life-giving Spirit; through Jesus Christ our Lord, who lives and reigns with you and the Holy Spirit, one God, now and for ever. Amen.

(*The Book of Common Prayer*, p. 222)

You've probably seen street preachers with their signboards.

> If you die tonight: Heaven (with pretty blue clouds) or Hell (with menacing flames)?

> "Life is short. Eternity isn't." —God

> Where are you sitting for eternity...smoking or non-smoking?

> Stop, drop, and roll does not work in Hell.

> If you think it's hot here, imagine Hell!

All of these slogans—and this way of seeing the world—place an emphasis on where you're going when you die. But these slogans have some fundamental flaws:

❖ Usually this viewpoint is trying to instill a sense of fear.

❖ It portrays belief in God or being a Christian as a means to an end.

❖ It's about where you go when you die.

❖ It's about getting your ticket to heaven.

The reason that these kinds of ads are so pervasive (and many would say so powerful) is that they tap into a common human concern. Most of us worry, or at least wonder, about what happens when we die.

Much of what we think about heaven and hell, and about the importance of either, comes not from the Bible or our faith but from popular culture. So let's see what the Bible actually says about hell and heaven.

When I say "hell", what do you envision? Flames; fire and brimstone? Down below, underground? The devil with a pointy tail? Circles of hell with punishment for different kinds of sinners? Darkness?

What do the scriptures say about hell? First of all, there are three words used that get translated as "hell."

IMAGES OF HELL FROM POPULAR CULTURE

- When you envision Satan as a serpent, you have Milton's *Paradise Lost* to thank for that.

- When you think of hell as a place where "the punishment fits the crime," you have Dante's *Inferno* to thank for that.

- The devil's pitchfork comes from Greek mythology; the halos of saints and angels are nowhere in the Bible but plentiful in art and iconography.

1. Sheol (Hebrew)

The only word in the Old Testament translated as hell or grave is *sheol*. This word is used sixty-five times in the Bible, all in the Old Testament.

> Drought and heat snatch away the snow waters; so does Sheol those who have sinned. (Job 24:19)

> They spend their days in prosperity, and in peace they go down to Sheol. (Job 21:13)

> Sheol beneath is stirred up to meet you when you come; it rouses the shades to greet you, all who were leaders of the earth; it raises from their thrones all who were kings of the nations. All of them will speak and say to you: "You too have become as weak as we! You have become like us!" Your pomp is brought down to Sheol, and the sound of your harps; maggots are the bed beneath you, and worms are your covering. (Isaiah 14:9-11)

> If I ascend to heaven, you are there; if I make my bed in Sheol, you are there. (Psalm 139:8)

Sheol is almost exclusively the realm of the dead—where all people (not just bad people) go when they die. Sometimes it is understood as a transitory place, where people go to await judgment (Isaiah 26:19, Daniel 12:2).

It does not contain a connotation that it is a "bad" place, where only bad people go, and there is no corresponding "good" place.

2. Hades (Greek, literally meaning "unseen")

This word is associated with Greek mythology, where *Hades* is both the name of the god of the underworld and also the name of the underworld/realm of the dead. When the Old Testament was translated into Greek, sheol became Hades. The concepts in the use of the two words are similar. When translated into English, Hades is sometimes translated as hell, sometimes death, and sometimes grave. This word is used eleven times in the Bible.

> For you have power over life and death; you lead mortals down to the gates of Hades and back again. (Wisdom 16:13)
>
> Where, O death, is your victory? Where, O death, is your sting? (1 Corinthians 15:55)
>
> Then Death and Hades were thrown into the lake of fire. This is the second death, the lake of fire; and anyone whose name was not found written in the book of life was thrown into the lake of fire. (Revelation 20:14-15)

Again, this is largely understood as the place where all people (not just bad people) go when they die.

3. Gehenna (Hebrew and Greek, literally meaning "the valley of Hinnom")

Gehenna was an actual, geographic place, originally the site of Baal worship (Jeremiah 32:35). It then becomes a garbage dump outside Jerusalem, where trash was perpetually burned. In the Old Testament, it is never translated as hell; instead it is typically rendered "Valley of Hinnom," describing the geographic location. In the New Testament, however, Gehenna is frequently translated as hell, even though to the original audience, it would have been a familiar place. Thus Gehenna functions largely like a metaphor rather than a literal identification (Mark 9:42-48, Matthew 10:28).

For many, the most iconic image of hell in the Bible, and the one that forms many of our assumptions about what hell is like, is the story of Lazarus and the Rich Man.

Lazarus and the Rich Man
Luke 16:19-31

There was a rich man who was dressed in purple and fine linen and who feasted sumptuously every day. And at his gate lay a poor man named Lazarus, covered with sores, who longed to satisfy his hunger with what fell from the rich man's table; even the dogs would come and lick his sores.

The poor man died and was carried away by the angels to be with Abraham. The rich man also died and was buried. In Hades, where he was being tormented, he looked up and saw Abraham far away with Lazarus by his side. He called out, "Father Abraham, have mercy on me, and send Lazarus to dip the tip of his finger in water and cool my tongue; for I am in agony in these flames." But Abraham said, "Child, remember that during your lifetime you received your good things, and Lazarus in like manner evil things; but now he is comforted here, and you are in agony. Besides all this, between you and us a great chasm has been fixed, so that those who might want to pass from here to you cannot do so, and no one can cross from there to us." He said, "Then, father, I beg you to send him to my father's house—for I have five brothers—that he may warn them, so that they will not also come into this place of torment." Abraham replied, "They have Moses and the prophets; they should listen to them." He said, "No, father Abraham; but if someone goes to them from the dead, they will repent." He said to him, "If they do not listen to Moses and the prophets, neither will they be convinced even if someone rises from the dead."

This passage is far from clear and raises some important questions. The word here is "Hades"—does this resemble some of the other verses about Hades? What about the mythological understanding of Hades?

> Our views of heaven are influenced more by popular culture than by the Word of God.

What about the "great chasm" between Hades and the unnamed place "with Abraham." Is this heaven? Abraham says no one can cross from one side to the other. Does Jesus' death and resurrection change this?

This is a parable told by Jesus (as indicated by "there was a rich man who" and other elements of a parable). Does knowing this is a parable and not a historical account affect how we understand hell as portrayed here?

What becomes apparent is that hell, as described in scripture, is not very clear at all. We don't know exactly what it is like. Is it eternal, or is it transitory? Examples from scripture and tradition support both perspectives. Does hell exist for punishment or purification? Does Jesus' death and resurrection change the reality of hell? What does it mean to say, in keeping with the belief of the early church as testified to in the Apostle's Creed, that Jesus "descended into hell"?

Lest we think that confusion is limited to hell, let's look at heaven.

When I say heaven, what do you envision? Streets paved with gold? Peter at the pearly gates? Comfort, happiness, peace? Doing things we love and enjoy? Our loved ones, just as we remember them?

Once again, we realize that our views of heaven are influenced more by popular culture than by the Word of God. Let's look at some biblical views of heaven.

The Hebrew word that is often translated as heaven in the Old Testament is *shamayim*, which means the "place in the sky where God lives." This is not a place where people go when they die, because in ancient Jewish understanding, people don't live where God lives. God lives in heaven, not us.

In the New Testament, much of the understanding of heaven echoes the Old Testament: heaven is where God is; heaven is where God lives. We add to the idea that heaven is where Jesus comes from and returns to (John 3:13; Acts 7:56). Jesus, by virtue of coming from heaven, dying, being resurrected, and returning to heaven (the place where God is), opens the passageway to heaven, the place where God is (John 6:35-40). Jesus thus opens the gates to heaven for humanity.

But what, precisely, is heaven like?

There are almost no actual descriptions of heaven in the scriptures. The streets of gold and pearly gates so often referenced in descriptions both come from the Revelation to Saint John (21:21). These descriptions are part of John's elaborate vision, which is full of poetic imagery and metaphor. Some of it is seriously trippy and is almost certainly not meant to be literal. Neither Revelation nor any other scripture describes heaven as a place focused on our comfort and happiness, on our enjoyment and leisure. Instead, every reference to heaven makes it clear that God is at the center of what's to come.

We learn several things from the scriptural view of heaven, and those things might surprise us.

❖ What will be most memorable about heaven is the nearness to God's presence. (Revelation 7:9-17)

❖ Our activity in heaven will not be playing games but rather joining with angels and archangels and all the company of heaven in the worship and praise of God. (Revelation 5:11-14)

❖ Heaven isn't just about us as individuals, or even the whole of humanity. Instead heaven is about everything: through Christ all creation is being redeemed. (Romans 8:19-23)

Though the vision of Revelation is not a literal description of what heaven is like, it gives us a good idea of what the central focus of heaven will be: God. God's praise, God's glory, God's presence.

So with few actual descriptions of heaven and hell and a lot of debate and open questions about what they are like—not to mention who goes where!—it would be

> The central focus of heaven will be God. God's praise, God's glory, God's presence.

easy to say forget it all and ignore both. But scripture and tradition both include hell and heaven; our creeds proclaim them, and we cannot ignore that Jesus talked about them both. We can't throw the baby out with the bathwater.

All descriptions of eternity include an aspect of God as judge. God is consistently described as a merciful judge, but we can't dismiss the reality that all of what we've done will be brought into the light of God's presence and that God says there will be consequences for the way we lived and treated one another in this world. And God's judgment is, in many ways, reassuring. Who would want to live in a world where there were no consequences for actions, where what we do didn't matter? When we understand that judgment is the time when the truth is spoken, all our life is brought into the light, and that God's love and mercy shines through it all, we perhaps begin to see God's judgment as something to be embraced rather than eschewed.

The Episcopal Church expresses our understanding of this clearly in the Catechism on page 862 of *The Book of Common Prayer*:

Q: What do we mean by heaven and hell?

A: By heaven, we mean eternal life in our enjoyment of God; by hell, we mean eternal death in our rejection of God.

While acknowledging the reality of God's judgment and affirming the historic faith in the reality of both heaven and hell, The Episcopal Church describes them in little detail, instead relying largely on mystery.

So what can we say about heaven and hell?

Though Jesus didn't describe heaven in detail, he talked about the kingdom of heaven or the kingdom of God a lot. Jesus speaks about the kingdom of heaven mostly in parables (Matthew 13:24-47). The kingdom of heaven is compared to a king giving a wedding banquet, a pearl of great price, a treasure hidden in a field, a net that catches many fish, a seed that is sown, or someone who sows seed. In the parables, the kingdom of heaven is usually valuable, worth giving everything for. It is something surprising. It is something both large and small, something that grows and multiplies exponentially.

Jesus tells us to pray for the kingdom of heaven to come (remember the Lord's prayer?).

Jesus repeatedly says that the kingdom of heaven is near —very near (Matthew 4:17, 10:7). Jesus actually goes even further and says that the kingdom of God is already here, that it is among us (Luke 17:20-21).

From the parables and Jesus' talk about the kingdom of heaven, we learn two incredibly important things. First, the details of the kingdom of heaven are mysterious, described most fully in poetry and metaphor and story. Second, the kingdom of heaven is not exclusively a place, removed from this world but is in some way already here, near, among us, and at hand.

The rest of the New Testament continues this understanding of heaven and the kingdom of heaven— that is it both mysterious and somehow something that is already here, that we already belong to (1 Corinthians 2:7-9, Ephesians 2:4-7, Ephesians 1:9-10, Philippians 3:20).

This begins to lead us to our transformed question. If we simply ask, "Where do I go when I die?" then we fall into a well of fallacies. We get bogged down in questions about the details of heaven and hell and what they are like, when so much of that is shrouded in mystery and metaphor. We start arguing about who is going where (as if we knew!) when scripture clearly proclaims God as the ruler and judge of all. We make eternity about us, when it is clearly and emphatically about God. And perhaps most distressingly, we spend our time focused on what is to come rather than living in the light of

> The Christian hope is about life, not just what happens after death.

the kingdom of heaven here and now. We would do better instead to focus on working out, with fear and trembling, our own salvation (Philippians 2:12).

Jesus and our tradition are both pretty clear that the important thing is not getting our ticket punched to heaven but about life here and now. Jesus spends a great deal of time talking about "salvation." While we may think that he means salvation at the end of time, what most people don't realize is that the idea of salvation, *sozo* in Greek, is about health, wholeness, fullness. Salvation is about life. It emphasizes not some future state but wholeness and fullness here and now, as well. Jesus does not say to the broken and suffering people who come to him, "It's okay. You'll be saved when you die." Jesus heals them here and now; he brings them to health and wholeness in this life. And he commands them to use that health and wholeness in service of God.

And when Jesus talks about "eternal life," he speaks of it not as a future possibility but as a current reality.

❖ "Very truly, I tell you, anyone who hears my word and believes him who sent me has eternal life, and does not come under judgment, but has passed from death to life" (John 5:24). Notice here the present tense verb: those who believe have eternal life, not they will have it in the future.

❖ "The thief comes only to steal and kill and destroy. I came that they may have life, and have it abundantly" (John 10:10). Jesus comes so that people can have abundant life. That is fullness of life, here and now.

We reiterate this reality in our words of administration at communion: "The body of our Lord Jesus Christ keep you in everlasting life." We pray—not to have everlasting life in the future, but to be kept in everlasting life—starting now and continuing into what is to come.

So instead of asking where we go when we die, perhaps we might borrow a different question from The Episcopal Church's Catechism instead. On page 861 of *The Book of Common Prayer,* the Catechism puts it this way:

Q: What is the Christian hope?

A: The Christian hope is to live with confidence in newness and fullness of life, and to await the coming of Christ in glory, and the completion of God's purpose for the world.

Completion implies that there is a beginning and that God is beginning that work even now—and bringing it to fulfillment at that ultimate day. It is the completion of God's purpose, not our purposes. It is the completion of God's purposes for the world: not just ourselves, not just humanity, but the whole world.

Though we have been given the promise of heaven in Jesus Christ, that promise alone is not our hope. According to our faith, earthly life is not some holding period, waiting to get our ticket stamped for the train to heaven. Our hope is not in heaven alone.

❖ The Christian hope is about life—not just what happens after death.

❖ The Christian hope is about living with confidence in newness and fullness and abundance of life—this life, here and now.

❖ The Christian hope is that the kingdom of heaven that Jesus proclaimed is here and now, in addition to there and then.

❖ The Christian hope is that heaven is a completion of what is already begun here and now.

❖ The Christian hope is that this completion will embody God's purpose for the world.

The Christian hope is a much bigger hope, a much richer promise, a much fuller reality, than just getting to go someplace nice when we die.

The kingdom of heaven, for Christians, is not a life or death choice; it is a life and death promise—the presence of God is here and now, made close in the coming of Jesus. We currently see that presence "through a glass darkly," but the promise of God is that we will, at length, at some unexpected day and hour in unexpected and unimaginable ways, see God face to face.

O God, who be the glorious resurrection of your Son Jesus Christ destroyed death and brought life and immortality to light: Grant that we, who have been raised with him, may abide in his presence and rejoice in the hope of eternal glory; through Jesus Christ our Lord, to whom, with you and the Holy Spirit, be dominion and praise for ever and ever. Amen.

(*The Book of Common Prayer*, p. 223)

Reflection questions

❖ What images of heaven and hell did you grow up with? Where did they come from?

❖ What images of heaven and hell do you now hold? Where did they come from?

❖ What is difficult for you in thinking about heaven and hell? What is comforting to you?

❖ How might it change your outlook to focus on the Christian hope, instead of where you will go when you die?

9

WHY DO I
NEED CHURCH?

Gracious Father, we pray for thy holy Catholic Church. Fill it with all truth, in all truth with all peace. Where it is corrupt, purify it; where it is in error, direct it; where in any thing it is amiss, reform it. Where it is right, strengthen it; where it is in want, provide for it; where it is divided, reunite it; for the sake of Jesus Christ thy Son our Savior. Amen.

(*The Book of Common Prayer*, p. 816)

When people find out I'm a priest, one of the responses I frequently get is, "Oh, I'm spiritual, but not religious." This is not surprising, given the largest growing religious affiliation in the US is "none." An astounding number of people say they are Christian but don't go to church. These no-church Christians have lots of reasons.

❖ I don't need to go to church; I connect with God on the golf course, in nature, etc.

❖ I tried church, but it didn't work for me.

❖ I didn't like the sermon or the music (or the people!).

❖ I was hurt by the church.

❖ I don't like the clergy.

❖ Christians are hypocrites.

❖ I'm just so busy.

Many of those reasons are valid, in some sense. They contain accurate critiques of the church and of "church people." However, if we're honest, all of them reflect misconceptions about what church is and what it is for.

Some operate out of a belief that "church=services." Then, if the worship service is flawed (or boring), there's no reason to go to church.

Some operate out of a belief that "church=a building." If that's true, then the church is just another building that might sometimes contain or point to God. There are, some will say, other equally valid places to meet God, like in nature or on golf courses.

> The Bible gives us a demanding account of what the Church is and should be.

Many people operate out of an understanding that "church=for me, for us." The purpose of church is making us feel good. Therefore, we stop going if church doesn't make us feel good, or if something else makes us feel better.

The biblical understanding of the Church bears little resemblance to a building, or a place that is just about services, or something that exists primarily for me. The Bible gives us a much richer and more demanding account of what the Church is and should be. The Bible describes for us Church with a big "C," the universal Church, the body of all the faithful, which is not about a building or worship services, an individual or even a single congregation.

The Bible uses a variety of images to describe the Church. Some of them are familiar to us, but many are surprising when we dig beneath the surface.

Holy Temple
Ephesians 2:22, 1 Peter 2:4-5, 9-10

One of the most obvious images for the Church is that it is a holy temple. We think we know this: that the Church is a building. But the only church building the New Testament talks about is one made, not of stones, but of people. Christians are "built together spiritually into a dwelling place for God" (Ephesians 2:22). We are, each of us, "living stones." The Church is not a building, in any traditional sense; it is a holy temple comprised of people. And this is fundamentally a corporate rather than an individual identity. One stone is not a building; it is simply a rock. It is only a collection of stones, built together intentionally into a structure, that comprise a temple.

This means that the Church is built in the gathering together of people. The Church is built through our presence together rather than through the construction of a particular place. It also means that, in the absence of individual people, the structure becomes unstable—there are "holes" in the wall when one living stone decides to stay home. The church building is just a building where we gather to be Church. The people, not the stones, form the Church.

Body of Christ
1 Corinthians 12:12-31, Romans 12:4-8

Another well-known image of the Church is that of the Body of Christ. The people of the Church are not individuals; they are members of a single body. This view emphasizes unity rooted in diversity. Like a human body, which requires hands, feet, lungs, ears, and many other parts to function, the church requires its different parts to function well. In the church, the different parts are various people called to various ministries. This is variety, not superiority. There is no "better" part or function; we are in it together. There is meant to be no competition.

In this model, we all need each other. None of us can say, "I have no need of you." We are literally maimed when we don't have one another, and our senses and actions are impoverished by the absence of a "member."

Consider the story of José María Olazábal, a professional golfer. One day he injured his foot, and this caused him to walk funny. His walk began to affect his back. His back pain affected his golf swing. His career never was quite the same again. What was a relatively minor injury, not properly healed, almost ruined his entire golfing career. One non-working part spoiled the body.

Our parts are connected. We are the Body of Christ, with many members. We must recognize that one member who is not healthy or functioning properly can impact many others in ways that are not obvious. We care for each other because we love each other. We must also realize that caring for each other is what keeps the whole body healthy.

Family or Household
Galatians 3:25-26, Galatians 4:4-7

The most pervasive metaphor for the Church in the New Testament is that of a family or household; the reference is usually implicit, by reference to God as a parent (Father or Mother) and us as God's children. The Church is a family because we are all related to God, our parent. We are also clearly called to be related to one another. We aren't family only by virtue of our relationship to God but by virtue of the way we relate to one another. "Brethren" or "brothers and sisters" are the most common words for Christians in the New Testament. The Church, then, is a collection of siblings.

I think this is the most misunderstood and abused understanding of what the Church is called to be. Typically, when I hear people say that their church is like a family, what they mean is that their church is a group of nice, like-minded people who always get along. Think about your family. Do any of these things accurately describe your experience of family?

❖ Is your family full of people who are always nice, who always accede to your every desire? Or is your family full of people who challenge and stretch you and tell you the truth even when it's really hard to hear?

❖ Is your family full of people who you agree with all the time, and do you always get along with them? Or is your family a group of people with a vast variety of viewpoints (so varied that you wonder how you could possibly be related to them) but to whom you are inextricably bound?

❖ Is your family full of people who you always, every day, like and are glad to see? Or is your family a group of people that you are bound and covenanted to love, even if you don't like them in that moment?

A Church is a family when it has wildly different people who don't always like each other, who have bad days and bad ways and yet somehow belong to one another anyway. A Church is like a family when it has a crazy Uncle Joe that everyone's a little embarrassed about, but they keep inviting him to family dinners anyway. A Church is like a family because we don't choose them, and some days the only thing that we share in common is that we are all chosen by God.

Light
Revelation 1:10-12, 20; Matthew 5:14-16

In the Revelation to Saint John, the image of a lampstand is used as a metaphor for the Church. John describes an elaborate vision in which seven lampstands are representative of seven churches. The idea is that the churches stand as God's light amidst the world. Churches carry the torch of the light of Christ (John 1:1-9). This is an image that Jesus himself uses too. In Matthew 5:14-16, we hear the familiar words: "You are the light of the world." The Greek "you" here is plural. It really says "y'all are the light of the world." This is not an individual identification akin to "This little light of mine, I'm gonna let it shine." It is the community, the gathering together, the Church, which is the light. The people (plural) together are the light (singular). If we're going to sing a song, it shouldn't be about my light but about God's light that we all share. "We are marching in the light of God." We are called and commanded to be a light that is not hidden but that is on a lampstand to "give light to all in the house."

If we listen to the images of the Church presented by scripture, then we begin to understand that the Church is far more than just worship services, or a building, or something that exists for us at all. In fact, the Church described in the Bible has little to do with any of those things. When we listen to the words of scripture, we stop asking, "Why do I need Church?" and instead begin asking, "What is my role in the Church?"

The Church is not simply a building, not only for worship services, not merely about me.

The Church is a Holy Temple of God. It is a place built out of its members, living stones, who gather together in praise and worship.

The Church is the Body of Christ. Teresa of Avila is often quoted, "Christ has no body but yours, No hands, no feet on earth but yours, Yours are the eyes with which he looks Compassion on this world, Yours are the feet with which he walks to do good, Yours are the hands, with which he blesses all the world." The Church is the primary expression of God's presence lived out in the world, the place where the rubber meets the road for God in our time.

The Church is the family of God. It is the group of people who are related both to God and one another. A popular campfire song has the refrain, "and they'll know we are Christians by our love." We show ourselves as the family of God when we love one another the way that Christ loved us (John 15:12-17).

The Church is a light in the world. Our light (not merely as individuals but as a community) stands as a testament to the Light of the World, Jesus Christ, who illuminates the darkness of this present time.

And church is not for me, for us, at all. In fact, the main thing we do at church isn't for us either. Worship is for God. Philosopher Soren Kierkegaard famously

> Too often we think of the church as a club for its members.

said that we get it wrong when we imagine that we who attend worship are the audience and the priest or God is the performer. Rather, in Kierkegaard's view, we are the performers, the priest is the one holding the cue cards, and God is the audience.

To put it yet another way, Philip Yancey writes,

> Church exists primarily not to provide entertainment or to encourage vulnerability or to build self-esteem or to facilitate friendships but to worship God; if it fails in that, it fails. I have learned that the ministers, the music, the sacraments, and the other "trappings" of worship are mere promptings to support the ultimate goal of getting worshippers in touch with God. If ever I doubt this fact, I go back and read the Old Testament, which devotes nearly as much space to specifications for worship in the tabernacle and temple as the New Testament devotes to the life of Christ. Taken as a whole, the Bible clearly puts the emphasis on what pleases God — the point of worship, after all.

> To worship, says Walter Wink, is to remember Who owns the house. (*Why Bother with Church?*)

Too often we think of the church as a club for its members. We like to be members of the club, and we want all the benefits. But maybe this view is 100 percent wrong too. Archbishop William Temple said that the church is "the only cooperative society in the world that exists for the benefit of its non-members." In church we worship God. And the mission of the church is not to benefit its members but to draw all people into the loving embrace of God. The Church, then, is not for us at all. It is for God: for God's worship, God's praise, God's glory and God's mission. And it is for others: for the whole world, for whom Jesus Christ gave his life and whom Jesus calls us, his followers, to love and serve.

Though the Church does not exist for us, that does not mean that we don't need the Church.

Saint John of the Cross offers a powerful image to remind us why we need the church, why we need each other: "The virtuous soul that is alone...is like the burning coal that is alone. It will grow colder rather than hotter." The Church offers the opportunity for us to gather together to fan our flame, to make the world brighter by combining our lights rather than dividing them. The Church challenges us to live the way that we are called to live, not because it feels good, but because it is what God is calling us to do.

Church often misses the mark

...the communion of sins, the forgiveness of saints...

I said at the beginning that many of the critiques offered against the Church are valid, and that is true. The Church often misses the mark. As individuals and as a community, we fail to do the things that we are called to do and to be the people we are called to be. But that doesn't mean that we give up.

There's a bumper sticker that reads: "Christians aren't perfect, just forgiven." The same could be said of the Church. The Church isn't perfect, just a community of people working out their salvation, relying on the forgiveness and grace of God.

A wise priest who taught me in seminary often told the story of a confirmation class he led. The students were required to recite the Apostles' Creed by heart. One of the boys, with a shaky voice, stood up at his turn. He got all the way through flawlessly. Then, at the end, as if in one breath, he said, "I believe in the Holy Spirit, the holy catholic Church, the communion of sins, the forgiveness of saints, the resurrection of the body, and the life everlasting."

The communion of sins, the forgiveness of saints. The priest sat for a moment in silence, as the boy stood awaiting judgment on whether or not he'd completed the assigned task. After a moment's thought, the priest said, "That's right.

That's just right." The boy had mixed it up, because the Apostles' Creed actually reads "the communion of saints, the forgiveness of sins," but maybe this other way of reading it isn't so far off the mark. Church is a gathering (a communion) of sinners, and it is a place where the saints (that's everyone who is baptized) can find forgiveness.

The holy catholic Church, the communion of sins, the forgiveness of saints.

So what if we understand the role of the Church as a Holy Temple, the Body of Christ, the Family of God, a Light in the World? What if we see the Church, not as perfect, but as the communion of sins and the forgiveness of saints? What if we see the Church not as for or about us, but for and about God and others? Then we might begin to ask, not "Why do I need Church?" but instead "What is my role in the Church?"

Which stone am I of God's Holy Temple? What part am I called to be in the Body? What indispensible function do I offer to the whole? Who are the members of my family, related whether I like it or not? How can I join my light to the lights of others that we might testify to the Light of the World?

Almighty God, you have built your Church upon the foundation of the apostles and prophets, Jesus Christ himself being the chief cornerstone: Grant us so to be joined together in unity of spirit by their teaching, that we may be made a holy temple acceptable to you; through Jesus Christ our Lord, who lives and reigns with you and the Holy Spirit, one God, for ever and ever. Amen. (*The Book of Common Prayer*, p. 230)

O God of unchangeable power and eternal light: Look favorably on your whole Church, that wonderful and sacred mystery; by the effectual working of your providence, carry out in tranquility the plan of salvation; let the whole world see and know that things which were cast down are being raised up, and things which had grown old are being made new, and that all things are being brought to their perfection by him through whom all things were made, your Son Jesus Christ our Lord. Amen. (*The Book of Common Prayer*, p. 291)

Reflection questions

❖ How does it change your understanding of Church to see it as for God or others, rather than for yourself?

❖ Which biblical understanding of the Church is most helpful for you, and why? Which is most difficult, and why?

❖ In what ways does our church fulfill the vision for Church that you heard tonight?

❖ In what ways does our church need to change in order to become the Church that God wants us to be?

❖ How would you answer the question, "What is my role in the Church?"

10

WHERE DO I
GO FROM HERE?

Almighty Father, whose blessed Son before his passion prayed for his disciples that they might be one, as you and he are one: Grant that your Church, being bound together in love and obedience to you, may be united in one body by the one Spirit, that the world may believe in him whom you have sent, your Son Jesus Christ our Lord; who lives and reigns with you, in the unity of the Holy Spirit, one God, now and for ever. Amen.

(*The Book of Common Prayer,* p. 255)

Hanging in the Museum of Fine Art in Boston is Paul Gaugin's famous triptych. It's a painting full of color and movement, large and imposing. Widely

> Where have we come from? What are we? Where are we going?

acknowledged as his masterpiece, the painting's title is inscribed in the upper left corner: *D'où Venons Nous/ Que Sommes Nous/Où Allons Nous*. Where have we come from? What are we? Where are we going? These are among the fundamental questions of human existence, and they frame our reflection in this final chapter.

Where have we come From?

Readers of this book have come from many places. Some came flush with faith, some full of doubt. Some have been church members for a long time; some are seekers brand new to this community. Some were looking for a refresher course; some were coming to hear these things for the first time. In this book, we have traveled together, asking questions of ourselves and our God and seeing those questions transform, even as the act of questioning transformed us.

❖ We asked whether it is possible to question our faith and found that questioning is an essential part of faith. As God-wrestlers like Jacob, we must learn how to question faithfully, holding on to God even as we struggle.

❖ We wondered who Jesus is, listening to the testimony of history, of faithful people through the ages, and of Jesus himself, and found ourselves ultimately confronted by the transforming question: "Who do you say that I am?"

❖ We asked why Jesus had to die and encountered a variety of metaphors for how Jesus has brought us back into relationship with God through atonement, choosing to die on the cross as a testimony to his great love for us.

❖ We wrestled with how we are called to live in light of Christ's love, exploring the laws of the Ten Commandments, the promises of our Baptismal Covenant, and the way the Holy Spirit empowers us to do things beyond our own capabilities.

❖ We learned how to read the Bible as God's Word, even when we aren't sure exactly what that means.

❖ We wondered whether God answers prayer and acknowledged the ways that we are called to engage in prayer, not merely to change God or the world but also to be changed ourselves.

❖ We wrestled with why bad things happen in this world and why evil exists. And we were reminded of Christ's presence with us always, even in the darkest of times and places.

❖ We explored the Christian understanding of afterlife: the reality of heaven and hell, the limits of our knowledge about either, and the call to live transformed lives here and now, even as we await the life that is to come.

> We are called to engage in prayer, not merely to change God or the world but also to be changed ourselves.

❖ We questioned why we need to go to church and found ourselves faced with the reality that Church is far more than a building and that we are called to take our place in the imperfect community of saints.

This little book has taken us on a journey, during which we have come through those questions, wrestling with them, even if some remain unanswered.

What are we?

In each chapter, we have learned something about what (and who) we are.

1. We are questioners, God-wrestlers, an identity not mutually exclusive with faithfulness.

2. We are Christians, those who bear the name of Jesus Christ, believing him to be who he says he is—both man and God.

3. We are saved, whatever metaphor we use to understand that salvation, by Jesus Christ who chose to die, for love of us.

4. We are people called to live in light of Christ's self-sacrificial love, empowered by the Holy Spirit to embody the reality of our baptismal promises in this world.

5. We are people of the Book, the Bible, understanding that the messy and difficult stories included in its pages are the Word of God.

6. We are people of prayer, bringing all of our lives, all of our hopes, hurts, love, and anger to God in holy conversation.

7. We are a light in the darkness, a living proclamation of God's love in the midst of the sin and brokenness of the world.

8. We are people of eternity, who live not in fear of hell but in the grip of Christian hope, which proclaims that we will all be judged by the God of mercy.

9. We are the Church, the Holy Temple, the Body of Christ, the Family of God, the Light of the World, flawed and broken but forgiven and holy, God's people just the same.

That's where we've come from. That is what and who we are. So now we must ask: Where are we going?

Where do I go from here?

We go forward, building on where we've come from, remembering what we are, as we move forward into where we are called to go and who we are called to become.

We must resist the temptation to say "whew, that's over with, I've finished this book" and move forward unchanged. We must resist the idea that we have "answered" the questions of faith or even asked all the questions of faith (we could have made this book twelve chapters or twenty-four, or 112—there are plenty more questions to ask!) The reality is that one of the most powerful images for the life of faith is that of a pilgrimage or journey.

Abraham's act of faith was to get up and go, beginning a lifelong journey with God.

> Now the LORD said to Abram, "Go from your country and your kindred and your father's house to the land that I will show you. I will make of you a great nation, and I will bless you, and make your name great, so that you will be a blessing. I will bless those who bless you, and the one who curses you I will curse; and in you all the families of the earth shall be blessed. So Abram went, as the

LORD had told him; and Lot went with him. Abram was seventy-five years old when he departed from Haran. Abram took his wife Sarai and his brother's son Lot, and all the possessions that they had gathered, and the persons whom they had acquired in Haran; and they set forth to go to the land of Canaan. When they had come to the land of Canaan, Abram passed through the land to the place at Shechem, to the oak of Moreh. At that time the Canaanites were in the land. Then the LORD appeared to Abram, and said, "To your offspring I will give this land." So he built there an altar to the LORD, who had appeared to him. From there he moved on to the hill country on the east of Bethel, and pitched his tent, with Bethel on the west and Ai on the east; and there he built an altar to the LORD and invoked the name of the LORD. And Abram journeyed on by stages towards the Negeb. (Genesis 12:1-9)

The call that Jesus issued to the disciples is the same call that he issues to all of us who believe in him: "Follow me." (Matthew 4:19, 8:22, 9:9, 16:24, 19:21, etc.). Part of our job as Christians is to continue on a lifelong journey of asking questions, reflecting on where we are and where we are going, wrestling with God and our faith.

This journey is not always straightforward—Abraham was not told his final destination, but he stepped forward in faith. The Israelites wandered in the desert for forty years, a circuitous journey of faith indeed. The disciples and the apostles found their journey taking them places they never imagined going, and they strayed from time to time.

> We continue on our journey, not always sure of where we are going, sometimes wandering, but pilgrims on the way, just the same.

So where do I go from here? We go on pilgrimage. We continue on our journey, not always sure of where we are going, sometimes wandering, but pilgrims on the way, just the same. We don't travel the road of the journey of faith ill-equipped. When we study a book like this, when we come and worship together, we receive tools for the journey. We pack our bags, if you will, with the things that we will need on our pilgrimage.

Tools for the Journey

We have, of course, the Bible, the beautiful, powerful book that tells the story of God's great love for us from before creation up to this very moment. The Bible, on its own, is an important tool in our backpacks. But sometimes (many times!) we might need some help reading and understanding the Bible.

❖ A good study Bible with notes is a great place to start. *The New Oxford Annotated Bible, HarperCollins Study Bible* and *New Interpreter's Study Bible* are all great options. Some people prefer a more contemporary rendering like *The Message*.

❖ *Introducing the New Testament* by Mark Powell.

❖ *An Introduction to the Old Testament* by Walter Brueggemann.

❖ *The Good Book* by Peter Gomes.

❖ *The Bible Makes Sense* by Walter Brueggemann.

We have *The Book of Common Prayer,* another resource in our library. The pages of *The Book of Common Prayer* are full of opportunities for prayer:

❖ The Daily Office (pp. 37-135)

❖ Daily Devotions for Individuals and Families (pp. 136-143)

❖ The Collects (pp. 159-261)

❖ Prayers and Thanksgivings (pp. 814-841)

But if we need help using *The Book of Common Prayer* or if we need guidance in other ways of praying, we have additional tools.

❖ Forward Movement publishes *Forward Day by Day,* a daily prayer resource that can be ordered in print or can be accessed by app or online.

❖ The website prayer.forwardmovement.org also includes the Daily Office—a great way to follow the ancient tradition of saying the Daily Office in modern form.

❖ *Prayer: Finding the Heart's True Home* by Richard Foster offers some other ways to pray.

We have as a tool the history of our faith, the tradition of what the Church has chosen to do through the ages and the way that tradition can strengthen and nourish today.

❖ *The Oxford Dictionary of the Christian Church* is an expansive dictionary of many of the terms of the church, with references.

❖ *The Story of Christianity* (Volumes 1 and 2) by Justo Gonzalez (HarperOne, 2010) is a great, readable, overview of Christian History.

❖ For something even more in-depth, *Christianity: The First Three Thousand Years* by Diarmaid MacCulloch (Viking Adult, 2010) is a long but excellent read.

The stories of the saints are a great place to learn and be strengthened in the faith; they are a witness to the work of God in Christ.

❖ Lent Madness (www.lentmadness.org) includes biographies, quotes, and kitsch from past saints. If it happens to be Lent, you can join in the madness, voting for your favorite saint in each matchup until someone is granted the golden halo.

❖ *Living Discipleship: Celebrating the Saints* (www.livingdiscipleship-fm.org) is an all-ages formation curriculum that engages in a year-long study of the saints.

We also have as a tool the practices of our faith—things like daily prayer and reading the Bible, sabbath time, and tithing. Those practices are like an exercise regime: the stretching and weight lifting we need to be able to walk this path every day. If you are looking for ways to integrate spiritual practices into your life, try:

❖ *Practicing our Faith* by Dorothy Bass.

❖ *The Heart of Christianity* by Marcus Borg.

❖ *Celebration of Discipline* by Richard Foster.

Additionally, if you have questions about an aspect of the Bible, faith, or church history, there are some surprising sources that can be helpful:

❖ Wikipedia.org is often a good place to start. Though you should crosscheck the information you find there, Wikipedia articles generally have good, basic information. Don't believe everything you read on Wikipedia but don't discount it out-of-hand either.

❖ The Episcopal Church's website has some information that might be helpful, including a glossary of terms that gives simple, succinct definitions: www.episcopalchurch.org/library/glossary

❖ Oxford University Press has a series of books called "A Very Short Introduction," which are quite good. They are very small and short, very readable, and address a variety of topics (e.g. *Jesus: A Very Short Introduction*). These books can be an excellent place to start.

❖ To go one step deeper, There's a great series of books published by Cowley Press, available on Amazon and at larger bookstores, called, "The New Church's Teaching Series."

And we don't go on this pilgrimage alone. We have companions on the journey. The community of faith—the disciples—were gathered as a group of twelve and traveled two by two. We, as Christians, are called to be companions to one another on the journey of life and the pilgrimage of faith.

> Therefore, since we are surrounded by so great a cloud of witnesses, let us also lay aside every weight and the sin that clings so closely, and let us run with perseverance the race that is set before us, looking to Jesus the pioneer and perfecter of our faith, who for the sake of the joy that was set before him endured the cross, disregarding its shame, and has taken his seat at the right hand of the throne of God. Consider him who endured such hostility against himself from sinners, so that you may not grow weary or lose heart. (Hebrews 12:1-3)

That's why it's so important for every Christian to have a faith community.

❖ Not a perfect one (there is no such thing!)

❖ Not one where you agree with everyone all the time (again, no such thing—and what fun would that be?)

❖ But an imperfect place where other imperfect people gather to be nourished and challenged and grow.

And for that to happen and work, every Christian must not only have a faith community but also be faithful to his or her community. Make the commitment to regular attendance and participation—even when it's hard or you don't feel like it. That's what it means to be a companion to others on this journey, and that's where you will find companionship on your own journey. In addition to the members of your congregation, your priest should be glad to talk to you about any questions that you have about your faith.

Above all, even when we feel most alone and far from our community of faith, we have another companion. We travel always with God in Christ, the one whom we follow.

> Every Christian must not only have a faith community but also be faithful to his or her community.

❖ Jesus, the one who loved us so much he was willing to come among us, to be incarnate, to be Emmanuel.

❖ Jesus, the one who promised to be with us always, even to the end of the age. (Matthew 28:20)

❖ Jesus who stretched out his arms of love on the hard wood of the cross for love of you, for love of me.

❖ That Jesus is also the one who walks with us along the way. (Luke 24:13-35)

So we travel onward in the pilgrimage of faith, a journey of questioning and questing and doubt. We travel, not always knowing where we are going, but well equipped, with packs full of the tools we need for the journey. We travel with companions, with the community of faith that surrounds and upholds us, the great cloud of witnesses, too many to number. And we travel always with Jesus, the Christ whose name we bear. So come on, let's go! The journey has just begun.

Almighty and eternal God, so draw our hearts to you, so guide our minds, so fill our imaginations, so control our wills, that we may be wholly yours, utterly dedicated to you; and then use us, we pray, as you will, and always to your glory and the welfare of your people; through our Lord and Savior Jesus Christ. Amen.

(*The Book of Common Prayer*, pp. 832-833)

Reflection questions

❖ What has been the most significant learning for you in this book?

❖ What questions are you still wrestling with as you continue on your journey?

❖ Which of the "tools" for the journey are you most excited about using, going forward? Which tools seem most intimidating?

❖ What help do you need from your companions as you continue on this journey?

RESOURCES

Faithful Questions can be a companion to *Transforming Questions,* a ten-session course designed to help participants engage the basic questions of the Christian faith through a combination of teaching and conversation. Participants gather to share a meal, which sets the foundation for fellowship. Scripture tells us again and again that people grow closer to God and one another through table fellowship, and that Christ becomes known to us in the breaking of bread. After the meal, a leader gives a presentation about a central question of the Christian faith. Then, in small groups, participants are invited into deeper reflection on and engagement with the question. Prayer both begins and ends each session to set the context for the conversations that occur within each class.

Facilitator and participant guides for *Transforming Questions* are available as downloads from Forward Movement. A printed participant's Book also is available from Forward Movement. To download or purchase, visit www.forwardmovement.org.

Learn more: www.transformingquestions.org

Books for further study

- *An Altar in the World* by Barbara Brown Taylor. HarperOne, 2010.

- *The Bible Challenge: Read the Bible in a Year* by Marek Zabriskie. Forward Movement, 2012.

- *Church: Why Bother?* by Philip Yancey. Zondervan, 2001.

- *The Creed: What Christians Believe and Why it Matters* by Luke Timothy Johnson. Image, 2007.

- *Crossing the Jordan: Meditations on Vocation* by Sam Portaro. Cowley Publications, 1999.

- *The Episcopal Handbook*. Morehouse Publishing, 2015.

- *Episcopal Questions, Episcopal Answers* by Ian Markham. Morehouse Publishing, 2014.

- *The Good Book: Discovering the Bible's Place in Our Lives* by Peter Gomes. HarperOne, 2002.

- *The Great Divorce* by C.S. Lewis. Geoffrey Bles, 1945.

FORWARD MOVEMENT RESOURCES

- prayer.forwardmovement.org
- *Welcome to The Episcopal Church*
- Other pamphlets and books available at www.forwardmovement.org

❖ *The Heart of Christianity: Rediscovering a Life of Faith* by Marcus J. Borg. HarperOne, 2004.

❖ *Heaven: Our Enduring Fascination with the Afterlife* by Lisa Miller. Harper Perennial, 2011.

❖ *Jesus: A Pilgrimage* by James Martin. HarperOne, 2014.

❖ *Jesus: A Very Short Introduction* by Richard Bauckham. Oxford University Press, 2011.

❖ *Jesus the Savior: The Meaning of Jesus Christ for Christian Faith* by William Placher. Westminster John Knox Press, 2001.

❖ *Let Your Life Speak: Listening for the Voice of Vocation* by Parker Palmer. Jossey-Bass, 1999.

❖ *Life Together* by Dietrich Bonhoeffer. Christian Kaiser Verlag, 1939.

❖ *Listening Hearts: Discerning Call in Community* edited by Suzanne Farnham. Morehouse Publications, 2011.

❖ *Love Wins* by Rob Bell. HarperOne, 2012.

❖ *Meeting Jesus Again for the First Time* by Marcus Borg. HarperCollins, 1994.

❖ *Mere Christianity* by C.S. Lewis. Geoffrey Bles, 1952.

❖ *Opening the Bible* by Roger Ferlo. Cowley Publication, 1997.

❖ *Practicing our Faith* by Dorothy Bass. Jossey-Bass, 2010.

❖ *Prayer: Finding the Heart's True Home* by Richard Foster. Zondervan, 2002.

❖ *Praying in Color* by Sybil MacBeth, *Writing to God* by Rachel Hackenberg, and other books in the Active Prayer Series. Paraclete Press, 2010.

❖ *The Problem of Pain* by C.S. Lewis. The Centenary Press, 1940.

❖ *The Secret Message of Jesus: Uncovering the Truth that Could Change Everything* by Brian McLaren. Thomas Nelson, 2007.

❖ *Simply Christian: Why Christianity Makes Sense* by N.T. Wright. HarperOne, 2010.

❖ *Surprised by Hope* by N.T. Wright. Zondervan, 2010.

❖ *Traveling Mercies: Some Thoughts on Faith* by Anne Lamott. Anchor Books, 2000.

❖ *Welcome to the Episcopal Church* by Christopher Webber. Morehouse Publishing, 1999.

❖ *When Bad Things Happen to Good People* by Harold Kushner. Anchor, 2004.

❖ *Where is God When it Hurts?* by Philip Yancey. Zondervan, 2002.

About the Authors

Scott Gunn is executive director at Forward Movement, a ministry of The Episcopal Church inspiring disciples and empowering evangelists. Before coming to Forward Movement, Scott was a parish priest in Rhode Island. Educated at Luther College, Yale Divinity School, and Brown University, he is passionate about travel, photography, and technology, along with working to reinvigorate the life of the church. He blogs at www.sevenwholedays.org.

Melody Wilson Shobe is an Episcopal priest who has served churches in Rhode Island and Texas. A graduate of Tufts University and Virginia Theological Seminary, Melody is currently working on curriculum development for Forward Movement. Melody, her husband, and their two daughters live in Dallas, Texas, where she spends her spare time reading stories, building forts, conquering playgrounds, baking cookies, and exploring nature.

About Forward Movement

Forward Movement is committed to inspiring disciples and empowering evangelists. While we produce great resources like this book, Forward Movement is not a publishing company. We are a ministry.

Our mission is to support you in your spiritual journey, to help you grow as a follower of Jesus Christ. Publishing books, daily reflections, studies for small groups, and online resources is an important way that we live out this ministry. More than a half million people read our daily devotions through *Forward Day by Day,* which is also available in Spanish (*Adelante Día a Día*) and Braille, online, as a podcast, and as an app for your smartphones or tablets. It is mailed to more than fifty countries, and we donate nearly 30,000 copies each quarter to prisons, hospitals, and nursing homes. We actively seek partners across the Church and look for ways to provide resources that inspire and challenge.

A ministry of The Episcopal Church for eighty years, Forward Movement is a nonprofit organization funded by sales of resources and gifts from generous donors. To learn more about Forward Movement and our resources, please visit us at www.forwardmovement.org (or www.AdelanteEnElCamino.org).

We are delighted to be doing this work and invite your prayers and support.